REDEEMING
AMERICAN
DEMOCRACY

REDEEMING AMERICAN DEMOCRACY

Lessons from the Confederate Constitution

MARSHALL L. DEROSA

PELICAN PUBLISHING COMPANY
GRETNA 2007

Library of Congress Cataloging-in-Publication Data

DeRosa, Marshall L., 1955-
  Redeeming American democracy : lessons from the Confederate
Constitution / Marshall L. DeRosa.
    p. cm.
  Includes bibliographical references and index.
  ISBN 978-1-58980-472-2 (hardcover : alk. paper) 1. State rights—
Confederate States of America. 2. Decentralization in government—
Confederate States of America. 3. Federal government—Confederate
States of America. 4. Constitutional law—Confederate States of America. 5.
State rights—United States. 6. Decentralization in government—United
States. 7. Federal government—United States. 8. Constitutional law—
United States. I. Title.
  KFZ9002.D49 2007
  342.73—dc22

                                                    2007020918

Printed in the United States of America
Published by Pelican Publishing Company, Inc.
1000 Burmaster Street, Gretna, Louisiana 70053

To Ross M. Lence (1943-2006), teacher, friend, and inspiration

CONTENTS

ACKNOWLEDGMENTS

This book has been a work in progress for several years. Two educational institutes have been especially instrumental in the publishing of this book: The Abbeville Institute (http://www.abbevilleinstitute.org/index.html) and Stephen D. Lee Institute (http://sdli.scv.org/index.php?F=1). The bringing together by these institutes of scholars and students interested in the South's contributions to the American experience is unique and critically needed if future generations are to appreciate and uphold the principles of 1776. Pelican Publishing Company's Milburn Calhoun, publisher and president, and Nina Kooij, editor in chief, are to be credited for too much to mention here. Suffice it to say that from surmounting the devastating effects of Hurricane Katrina to sorting out the dense linguistics of academia, this book has come to print due to their valiant professional efforts. And lastly, but not in importance, my wife Mary's support in all things is a gift for which I will forever be grateful.

INTRODUCTION

I believed that you were fighting the battles of our liberty, our progress and our civilization; and I mourn for the stake which was lost at Richmond more deeply than I rejoice over that which was saved at Waterloo.   Lord Acton to Robert E. Lee, 1866

❧   I   ❧

The Confederate States of America (CSA) and democracy at first glance appear to be inimical concepts. Such is not the case. The common thread between them is political centralization. The thesis that follows is that the model of government embodied in the CSA is highly conducive to American democracy and commensurately resistant to political centralization, the backbone of political tyranny. The more political power is centralized, the greater the capacity of a central government to impose an arbitrary rule on its subjects.

Democracy in the American tradition is best explained as a government based upon the consent of the governed within a federal republic, not simplistic national or state majority rule. American democracy places constraints on majorities and minorities, constraints that are adumbrated in the United States (US) and state constitutions. Within this system, majority rule is more potent at the state than the national level. James Madison's primary justification for replacing the Articles of Confederation and Perpetual Union was that under it the States were too democratic and thereby interfering with national interests. He argued that state governments were made too unstable by the "superior force of an interested and overbearing majority." The resulting instability created by the state majorities needed to be fixed. The fix was to shift certain policy responsibilities away from the States and to the national government.[1] The States reserved the bulk of their powers and delegated to the US government only those powers deemed to be in the collective interests of the States. Those collective interests included national security and commerce, i.e., trade, among the States.

As a result, and due in large measure to the States' rights Anti-Federalists,[2] the US Constitution maintained a decentralized form of government. As was the case under the Articles of Confederation, the States retained their sovereignty and still did most of the governing, excepting those governing duties delegated to the national government. But soon after the Constitution's ratification, decentralization began to give way to the pressures of centralization. Lacking a clear demarcation between national and state governing responsibilities, the nationalists initially at the helm of the national government began to expand its powers ever so slightly. US Supreme Court case law regarding national legislative and judicial supremacy over the States manifested the creeping expansion of national power. By 1865 the creep was an all-out sprint and the substantial 1789 constitutional barriers to centralized national power were for the most part buried in the dust along with the CSA. The Confederacy's demise took with it meaningful States' rights and its prerogatives of nullification, interposition, and secession. American democracy was left orphaned and subject to the abuse of a manipulative, self-serving, and power-hungry nationalism.

The CSA framers were very much aware of the US government's insatiable appetite for power. They not only anticipated the irrepressible rise of US centralized political power, but for their new country designed a model of government to prop up and strengthen the 1789 barriers against centralization. But the Confederates were defeated and their decentralized model of government, both its operation and its place in the world of ideas, was crushed under the weight of defeat. Following the defeat of the CSA, centralization continued unabated, not only heedless of States' rights but increasingly heedless of national rights. As States have been reduced to serving as administrative agents of the national government, stripped of their sovereignty and dignity, the United States is on track to become an administrative agent of transnational governing bodies, e.g., transnational trade organizations such as GATT, NAFTA, and CAFTA, the SPP,[3] and the United Nations, in the emerging new world order.

The centralization process was essential to the development of the nation-state, but autonomous from it. The nation-state served as the means, not the end, of centralization. The creation of the nation-state was designed to serve the objective of subordinating organizations and institutions that compete for the allegiances of individuals. In other words, the nation was the product of a power struggle. For example, in feudal times, centers of political power such as the Church and regionally autonomous feudal lords competed with the monarch for the allegiances of individuals by providing for their spiritual and temporal needs. This continued up to the French Revolution, culminating in Napoleon, the personification of French nationalism. The French Revolution witnessed in France the final subordination of the Church and nobility as viable political competitors. The centralized bureaucratic French Republic was created as a means to consolidate power. Individuals were increasingly conditioned to turn to the centralized government for their spiritual and temporal needs, moving closer to the Rousseau model, in which individual wills were merged into a nationalized general will. The nationalized French general will culminated in centralized power, which triumphed over decentralized local and regional powers.[4]

As the general will subsumes local and regional wills into its vortex, the momentum for expansion is fueled by individuals becoming increasingly dependent on and demanding of the central government for their needs, both emotional and physical. What was true for the French Republic was true for Franklin Delano Roosevelt's New Deal, and is true for ongoing expansion of the national government's role in American life. European nations are undergoing a similar transformation. The European Court of Human Rights recently endorsed "the general interest of society to avoid the emergence of parallel societies based upon separate philosophical convictions and the importance of integrating minorities into society." The parallel society in question was a Christian community wanting to home school its children, which is essentially disallowed in the Federal Republic of Germany on the grounds that the Christian community deviates from the German/European secularized general will.[5]

In response to the centralizing policies of the New Deal, the foremost authority on community Robert Nisbet wrote that "the favorite strategy of proponents of the national community [general will], is to draw up a purportedly heartrending account of the disappearance of all the traditional communities such as kinship, neighborhood, church, and voluntary association of every kind, and then with majestic finality declare the national community [general will] to be our only salvation."[6] Realizing that political centralization was the path to tyranny, Nisbet insisted that "it should be the prime business of any serious conservative party or other faction to expose the fraudulence of such a phrase as national community."[7]

If a national central government with extensive powers results in the merger of society into the state, then what are the prospects that a transnational centralized government will be respectful of the traditional rights of life, liberty, and property? What are the prospects that in the emerging world order a hypercentralized government, presiding over the "interests" of the human family, will defer to traditional American communities and their fundamental right to be self-governing? Any model of political centralization that makes probable the personages of a Napoleon, a Lincoln, or a UN general secretary with comparable executive powers is incompatible with traditional notions of American democracy and its counterpart, genuine community self-determination—i.e., States' rights.

Lord Acton understood the dangers of centralization and in a letter to Gen. Robert E. Lee clearly expressed the Confederacy's hope to protect society from the encroaching control of the state:

Without presuming to decide the purely legal question, on which it seems evident to me from Madison's and Hamilton's papers that the Fathers of the Constitution were not agreed, I saw in State Rights the only availing check upon the absolutism of the sovereign will, and secession filled me with hope, not as the destruction but as the redemption of Democracy. The institutions of your Republic have not exercised on the old world the salutary and liberating influence which ought to have belonged to them, by reason of those defects and abuses of principle which the Confederate Constitution was expressly and wisely calculated to remedy. I believed that the example of that great Reform would have blessed all the races of mankind by establishing true freedom purged of the native dangers and disorders of Republics. Therefore I believed that you were fighting the battles of our liberty, our progress and our civilization; and I mourn for the stake which was lost at Richmond more deeply than I rejoice over that which was saved at Waterloo.[8]

❧ II ❧

The cliché "to the victor belong the spoils" includes articulating the justifications for and consequences of war. This is particularly the case in what is known as the American Civil War. That war unlike any other US war had to avoid being depicted as a war of conquest, for the simple reason that to do so would undermine the notion that the United States is a system of government based upon the consent of the governed. If the forceful subjugation of the CSA by the US were discovered to be a war of conquest, a war of economic and cultural imperialism of the North over the South, the myth that the US is a government based upon the consent of the governed would be exposed. Pres. Abraham Lincoln's status as the *vox populi* incarnate would be absurd. Lincoln would be acknowledged as the leader of regionally based interests battling against the self-determination of Southern States. Pres. Jefferson Davis would be conferred the mantle of George Washington minus the military victories requisite to Southern independence. In other words, the US national government's legitimacy would be exposed as predicated upon coercion, as a tyranny that crushed self-government of the Southern people. The political universe subsequently turned somewhat upside down.

Once the magnitude of the stakes is appreciated one can more readily understand why the officially recognized accounts of that war, as manifested in political socialization from elementary schools to the rhetoric of the national elite, is adhered to with such tenacity. Through political socialization, the American public is increasingly being trained to view the CSA as a repulsive abomination. Because the CSA framers and their principles of government pose the most serious challenge to political centralization, wielders of centralized power have little tolerance for those men and their decentralization principles.

The truth of the matter is that a rejection of CSA constitutional principles is a rejection of the 1776 revolutionary principles. The stakes are extremely high, as expressed by Alexander Hamilton in 1788, when he discreetly wrote in the aftermath of that earlier American revolution that it has been "reserved to the people of this country, by their conduct and example, to decide the important question, whether societies of men are really capable or not of establishing good government from reflection or choice, or whether they are forever destined to depend for their political constitutions on accident and force."[9]

It is the contention of this book that Hamilton's question has been answered, "to the general misfortune of mankind,"[10] and that the original and ongoing campaign against CSA principles is a ruse to augment the scope and reach of a coercive centralized government, at the expense of individual and community self-determination. The discerning Alexis de Tocqueville anticipated as much when he wrote:

> After having thus successively taken each member of the community in its powerful grasp, fashioned him at will, the supreme power then extends its arm over the whole community. It covers the surface of society with a network of small complicated rules, minute and uniform, through which the most original minds and the most energetic characters cannot penetrate to rise above the crowd. The will of man is not shattered, but softened, bent and guided; men are seldom forced by it to act, but they are constantly restrained from acting. Such a power does not destroy, but it prevents existence; it does not tyrannize, but it compresses, enervates, extinguishes, and stupefies a people, till each nation is reduced to be nothing better than a flock of timid and industrial animals, of which government is the shepherd.—I always thought that servitude of the regular, quiet, and gentle kind which I have just described might be combined more easily than is commonly believed with some of the outward forms of freedom and that it might even establish itself under the wing of the sovereignty of the people.[11]

If the 1830s of Tocqueville days manifested such tendencies, how much more so is the case today, with a national government that has few checks to effectively constrain its domestic and foreign policy objectives, and one that no serious thinker contends is effectively "under the wing of the sovereignty of the people"?

This is not meant to imply that the constitutional system of checks and balances, separation of powers, federalism, elections, fundamental rights, etc., properly maintained is antithetical to popular sovereignty. As a practical matter, to expect popular sovereignty under current conditions is unrealistic. With the size and scope of the national government, e.g., trillions of dollars in debt, a multitrillion-dollar annual budget, a legislative and bureaucratic apparatus churning out innumerable and incomprehensible legislative and administrative laws, along with its imperialistic designs to spread the same system abroad, it is little wonder that popular sovereignty has been buried under the sheer weight of centralized government. The CSA was designed to prevent this sort of corrupting centralization in a federal system. Just as the American Revolution of 1776 was a reactionary revolution to restore English rights long practiced by the colonies that were under assault by the English Parliament in the 1760s and 1770s, the Confederate revolution of 1861 was a reactionary revolution aimed at the restoration of American democracy as embodied in the Constitution of 1789.[12]

❧ III ❧

This book is an analysis of the so-called American Civil War's long-term impact on American democracy. Hard questions need to be openly discussed, as difficult as that is in today's political climate. Such questions have been contemplated and given a wink and a nod here and there. But the fact of the matter is that scholarship on the 1861 constitutional crisis is increasingly pro-Union. Pro-Confederate positions that secession was constitutional and Lincoln war policies both unconstitutional and unjust are tenable as long as the respective sides tolerate each other. But such tolerance is quickly waning as the symbols of the nineteenth-century Confederate mindset (such as its heroes, literature, flags, and constitutional preferences, i.e., genuine States' rights) are being attacked and erased from the American consciousness by ideologically motivated centralizers.

Scholarship has often been didactic and purposeful. One may conclude that effective scholarship placed in the service of the *polis* stems from interpreting complex events with the author's insights sprinkled throughout. Such insights may be available to readers with varying capabilities, astutely placed (or—more precisely—obscured) by the scholar according to the readership being addressed. Rather than simply a recorder of facts, a highly skilled scholar combines the qualities of the philosopher, political scientist, and historian. The historian functions as the recorder of facts; the philosopher is concerned with permanent things, such as justice, natural right, and human nature; and the political scientist skillfully applies the products of the historian and insights of the philosopher to the political realm, thereby making the efforts of the historian and philosopher not exercises in futility but with results.

Thucydides, for example, was neither exclusively a historian nor a philosopher per se, but rather a political scientist who wrote his war story to promote what he perceived to be the interests of Athens.[13] The same could be said about the role of political science and the war between the States. That reasonable people adamantly differ about the details, e.g., was Lincoln a crassly opportunistic politician or a saintly statesman, is more attributable to ideological disagreements about whether America's national character should be predominantly decentralized (States' rights) or centralized (empire). The point is that the quest for power is effectively choking off meaningful discourse about the relevance of the CSA in contemporary culture and politics, not because the CSA is irrelevant, but because it is too relevant.

Does scholarship about the Confederacy have a contribution to make to the twenty-first century? More specifically, are the core 1789 constitutional democratic principles embodied in the Confederate States of America, and, if so, are they relevant to Americans' public interests in the twenty-first century? Implicit in these questions is the very survival of a constitutionalism predicated upon the consent of the governed, as opposed to a form of government under the exclusive control of unaccountable and self-serving elites.

Admittedly, the American democracy and the *Confederate States of America* are concepts that appear to be strange bedfellows. Most would consider democracy to be the lifeblood of the American body politic, whereas the CSA has been depicted as an anti-democratic, metastasizing, cancerous tumor to be painfully extirpated, a process that began at Fort Sumter and continues to this day. It is assumed that the United States government and Lincoln were committed to democracy, and therefore justified in preserving the Union at all costs, whereas the CSA rested upon crass legalism in justification for the establishment of an oppressive system of labor sustained by the illegitimate CSA state governments. The official pro-Union version seeks to explain a very complex period of national development by draping the Northern States, the Republican Party, and President Lincoln with a cloak of justice and self-righteous indignation, and the CSA and its leaders with one of injustice and shame. But the commitment of the CSA to democratic principles was second to none and certainly surpassed that of Lincoln. If the lifeblood of the CSA was government based upon the consent of the governed, what does this reveal about the principles around which the CSA was built and subsequently crushed? Or more specifically, what does the CSA reveal about twenty-first-century America and its receptiveness towards transnational government?[14]

The US Supreme Court is not a reliable source for clarification about these issues. The Court's failure to recognize the legitimacy of the CSA and its state governments was a political necessity for centralization, but a constitutional swindle. Through its refusal to acknowledge a state's constitutional right to secede and its claim that the CSA was the product of "revolutionary violence" and "armed resistance to the rightful authority of the sovereign," the Court declared the legislative, executive, and judicial branches established throughout the CSA as nullities and lacking in any rightful authority.[15] In other words, as there were neither democratically elected governments nor rule of law in the CSA, but only the illegitimate rule of rebels, Lincoln's armies were justified in crushing "the rebellion." But in reality, what Lincoln's armies crushed was the constitutional rule of law, unprecedented in Western civilization.

But secession and the CSA and its state governments were functioning realities, based upon the same republican principles embodied in the Declaration of Independence (a secession document) and the 1789 US Constitution. The Confederate courts were integral parts of that once functioning republic, particularly in regard to the American rule of law, the bulwark of American democracy.

The premise of this book is that the CSA model of government is the dagger that needs to placed in the heart of the centralization essential to the emerging new world order, if the fundamental rights and liberties of 1789 are to be recovered and preserved. Hence, the CSA is juxtaposed to the new world order with the knowledge that the former is solidly grounded in, and an improvement of, the 1789 US Constitution, while the latter is the instrument through which the centralized rule of global elites claims to represent the human family's general will with public policy agendas procedurally and substantively antithetical to the principles of 1789.

Chapters 1 ("CSA Constitution"), 2 ("Confederate Justice"), and 3 ("Executive Power") will make manifest that the CSA was well within and an improvement upon the democratic principles of 1789; chapter 4 ("Liberty or Union") adumbrates the twenty-first-century developments that are culminating in a new world order destructive of those principles; and chapter 5 ("Secession: Liberty's Safeguard") discusses what can be done to recover what was won at Yorktown and lost at Appomattox.

REDEEMING
AMERICAN
DEMOCRACY

Chapter I

CSA CONSTITUTION[1]

I do not regard the failure of our constitutional Union, as very many do, to be the failure of self-government; to be conclusive in all future time of the unfitness of man to govern himself. Our State governments have the charge of nearly all the relations of personal property. This Federal Government was instituted mainly as a common agent for foreign purposes, for free trade among the States, and for common defense.

Sen. Jefferson Davis, January 10, 1861, US Senate

✂ **I** ✂

As Southern States seceded from the Union, they did not reject unionism per se. They realized that the benefits of membership in a voluntary union were substantial. They were also convinced that the Union from which they recently seceded provided the constitutional blueprint to structure a new union, or confederacy, of States. Most scholarship about the CSA considers the acceptance of the 1789 constitutional blueprint as evidence that Southern secession was merely the result of sour grapes stemming from their declining influence in national politics.[2] The rules of the political game were fine (i.e., the US Constitution); they just wanted a new set of players so that Southern political interests would dominate in the newly organized confederacy. According to this view, the CSA constitution is dismissed as a copy of the US Constitution with some minor editorial changes.

It is true that much of the CSA Constitution is a verbatim copy of the US Constitution, but it is also true that the structural and wording deviations from the US Constitution have profound implications for the depth and breadth of national powers vis-à-vis the States. As all schoolchildren know, the US Supreme Court has pedantically scoured

23

the structure and wording of the US Constitution in order to legit-imize ever expanding aspects of centralized governmental power. Upon close scrutiny, the deviations from the US Constitution to be found in the CSA Constitution substantively limit juridical options that favor centralized power over States' rights. The CSA Constitution strengthened the constraints on the national government's capacity to expand beyond the consent of the States. A close analysis of the CSA Constitution makes clear that it constrains, along the lines of John C. Calhoun's concurrent majority,[3] centralized authority within the con-fines of a confederate model based upon predominant States' rights. In short, the CSA Constitution limits centralized power much more effectively than does the US Constitution.

The Preamble of the CSA Constitution

The CSA Constitution's preamble contains four substantive qualifica-tions to the US Constitution's preamble. First, it affirms that the people of the Confederacy ordained and established the CSA Constitution through their respective States, "each State acting in its sovereign and independent character." The US Supreme Court has dubiously main-tained that the US Constitution was ordained and established by the American people, not the States. Although Article VII of the US Constitution requires the ratification of the conventions of nine States, the conventions were deemed by advocates of centralized power to be state-based forums for the collective action of the American people. For example, in 1798 Chief Justice Samuel Chase, in rejecting the "omnipo-tence of a state legislature," declared that the "people of the United States erected their constitution or forms of government, to establish justice, to promote the general welfare, to secure the blessings of liber-ty, and to protect their persons and property from violence."[4] Even the pro-States' rights Justice James Iredell let down his guard when he con-curred that it "has been the policy of all the American states, which have, individually, framed their state constitutions, since the revolution, and of the people of the United States, when they framed the federal constitution, to define with precision the objects of legislative power, and to restrain its exercise within marked and settled boundaries."[5]

According to this ahistorical view, the US Constitution ordained and established by the people of the nation places the American people as supreme over the people within their respective States. Accordingly, if a state is not the source of authority (i.e., a principal), it cannot withdraw that authority from the national government when its interests dictate that it should. The independence and sovereignty of each state, as expressed in both the Declaration of Independence and the Articles of Confederation, have been thereby swallowed up by the aggregation of the American people. Because the American people are sovereign, only the American people can release a portion of itself, i.e., the people within a particular state or States, from the contractual obligations of membership in the Union.

Building upon this distorted view of the supremacy of the American people over the States, President Lincoln announced in his first inaugural address that he would base his administration's legitimacy on the policy preferences of the American people, not the States. He insisted that "the Chief Magistrate derives all his authority from the people."[6] He viewed the fracturing of the Union not as a division between Northern and Southern States but as a division between the American people of the North, the majority, and the American people of the South, the minority. For Lincoln and his Republican Party, the breakup of the Union would be resolved "by the judgment of this great tribunal—the American people."[7] This approach gave his war policy the political cover it needed to coercively hold the Union intact, over the objections of Southern States.

Second, the CSA preamble recovers the traditions of the Declaration of Independence, the Articles of Confederation, and an original view of the US Constitution that the States are the sources of authority for the national government.[8] The CSA framers deleted the phrases "provide for the common defense" and "promote the general Welfare," in order to particularize the document's application to the States, in contrast to a general application to the American people. Whereas the US preamble reads, "We the People of the United States," the CSA preamble reads, "WE, the People of the Confederate States, *each State acting in its sovereign and independent character*" (emphasis added), which reaffirms that the sovereign States, not the people of the CSA, are the principals and the CSA government their agent. The preamble and Article I, section 8, clause 1, lack the "general Welfare" as an objective of the CSA. The central government was not charged with promoting the general welfare of the American people, the States notwithstanding, but the collective welfare of the States and, indirectly through the States, the welfare of the people within the CSA. The "common defense" of the States is a responsibility of the CSA Congress and is noted accordingly in Article I, section 8, clause 1, of the CSA Constitution. However, the common defense of the States, separate from the general welfare mandate, has a much narrower scope, i.e., protection against foreign powers, whereas the general welfare could be understood to include any public policy arguably beneficial to the nation as a whole, e.g., government-funded railroads.

Third, the purpose of the CSA Constitution was to form a "permanent federal government," not a "more perfect Union." Representing the nationalist interpretation of the US Constitution, President Lincoln equated a perfect Union with an indissoluble and perpetual Union. The title of the Articles of Confederation is: "Articles of Confederation and perpetual Union between the states of New Hampshire, Massachusetts-bay Rhode Island and Providence Plantations, Connecticut, New York, New Jersey, Pennsylvania, Delaware, Maryland, Virginia, North Carolina, South Carolina and Georgia." Lincoln asserted that the transition from the Articles of Confederation, which established a "perpetual Union," to the US Constitution, which established a "more perfect Union," necessitated a perfectly perpetual, indissoluble Union. In his inaugural address, he put the Southern States on notice that "if destruction of the Union, by one, or by a part only, of the States, be lawfully possible, the Union is *less* [emphasis added] perfect than before; the Constitution having lost the vital element of perpetuity." His formula, however, is fundamentally flawed. As the CSA framers insisted, a perfect Union is one that is based upon the consent of its members, the States. Accordingly, the permanent CSA federal government stemmed from a consensual agreement among the States to join the CSA. If a state were to withdraw its consent, the union between that state and the CSA would be dissolved. If all the States were to withdraw their consent, the CSA government would by default cease to exist. Under Lincoln's view, only a majority of the American people could dissolve the Union. A minority of the American people in a particular state were at the mercy of the national numerical majority.

The CSA framers made the Lincoln view untenable: (a) the States individually and voluntarily acceded to the CSA delegated powers to realize certain policy objectives shared with the other States (e.g., to form a permanent federal government, establish justice, ensure domestic tranquility, and secure the blessings of liberty); (b) States are subject to the jurisdiction of the CSA government's delegated powers while members of the CSA; (c) a state's secession from the CSA placed the seceded state outside the jurisdiction of the CSA's delegated powers; and (d) a union of States coercively maintained against the consent of its members would be a very imperfect union of States.

And fourth, the preamble invokes "the favor and guidance of Almighty God." Such an invocation is not necessarily consistent with the thrust of abolitionism, which placed its faith in the higher law of human reason. The fact that the CSA framers prayed for God's favor and guidance manifested a dependence on Divine Will and subordination to Divine Providence. Through their respective States, Southerners had a covenant with the Divine that had conditions attached. The terms of association among the States are articulated in the CSA Constitution, which is subordinated to biblical mandates to submit to God's guidance. God's guidance is not to be found in burning bushes or latter-day prophets, but in the text of the Bible. To deviate from the constitutional mandates was to break one's word and act in bad faith. Such behavior had consequences, such as the withdrawal of Divine favor. Because the transcendental order is directly incorporated into the CSA Constitution, with God as a guarantor of its terms, it is more than a legal obligation compulsively enforced. It is a covenant among the States contingent upon their willingness to morally and ethically interact with one another.[9] The motto of the CSA, Deo Vindice (God will vindicate), is an expression of the CSA's reliance on Divine Law in maintaining the permanency of the CSA. As evidenced by the recent refusal to include a reference to Europe's Judeo-Christian roots in the European Union Constitution's preamble, such omissions are not trivial matters.[10]

The Tenth Amendment

Article I, section 1, of the US Constitution stipulates that "all legislative Powers herein granted shall be vested in a Congress of the

United States, which shall consist of a Senate and House of Representatives." In the CSA Constitution, the powers are not *granted,* but *delegated.* Jurisprudentially, there is an important difference between granted powers and delegated powers. This is made clear in the landmark case *McCulloch v. Maryland* (1819), through which Chief Justice John Marshall conferred on the national government expansive legislative powers over the States.

In that opinion, Chief Justice Marshall promotes the centralized view of the Constitution by insisting that it was created by the American people, not the States. He argued that the States preceded the US Constitution and that the people of the States delegated to their state governments certain powers. Because those powers were delegated, the people in their respective States had the option to recall those powers from their respective state governments and re-delegate them to the state conventions. The American people, through their state conventions, then granted those powers to the newly formed US government. Delegated powers could be recalled, whereas granted powers could not. Marshall wrote in his opinion:

> The powers of the general government, it has been said, are delegated by the States, who alone are truly sovereign; and must be exercised in subordination to the States, who alone possess supreme dominion. . . . It has been said, that the people had already surrendered all their powers to the State sovereignties, and had nothing more to give. But, surely, the question whether they may resume and modify the powers granted to government does not remain to be settled in this country. Much more might the legitimacy of the general government be doubted, had it been created by the States. The powers delegated to the State sovereignties were to be exercised by themselves, not by a distinct and independent sovereignty, created by themselves. To the formation of a league, such as was the confederation, the State sovereignties were certainly competent. But when, "in order to form a more perfect union," it was deemed necessary to change this alliance into an effective government, possessing great and sovereign powers, and acting directly on the people, the necessity of referring it to the people, and of deriving its powers directly from them, was felt and acknowledged by all.[11]

According to Marshall, constitutional powers granted to the nation cannot be recalled by a state, because such powers were not delegated by a state but granted by the American people assembled in the state-based conventions. The American people would have to act en masse via a national constitutional convention in order to recall granted powers: "The government of the Union is a government of the people; it emanates from them; its powers are granted by them; and are to be exercised directly on them, and for their benefit. The government of the Union, though limited in its powers, is supreme within its sphere of action; and its laws, when made in pursuance of the constitution, form the supreme law of the land."[12]

Granted powers denote the voluntary transfer "with or without compensation" of "a gift or bestowal by one having control or authority over it."[13] In the case of those powers granted by the American people to the Congress, those powers are now in the possession of the Congress, and the people in their respective States have relinquished all rights of recalling those powers. Hedging their bets, in 1791 the States insisted upon the Tenth Amendment's reference to delegated powers, which merely empowers the Congress to perform tasks on behalf of the States as their agent.[14] Delegating powers to the Confederate Congress is much more consistent with States' rights than granting powers, because the former can be recalled by the States whereas the latter, according to US Supreme Court precedent, cannot be recalled.

The Tenth Amendment to the US Constitution stipulates that "the powers not delegated to the United States by the Constitution, nor prohibited by it to the States, are reserved to the States respectively, or to the people." The CSA Tenth Amendment equivalent stipulates that "the Powers not delegated to the Confederate States by the Constitution, nor prohibited by it to the States, are reserved to the States, respectively, or to the people thereof."[15] The "thereof" emphasizes that the CSA is a government of the States, that it emanates from them, and that its powers are delegated by them. Indeed, CSA powers are exercised directly on the Confederate people, but with States as the guardians as to how those powers are to be exercised. The wording "or to the people thereof" in the CSA Constitution clarifies that the American people do not constitute an alternative repository of power to the States.

The CSA Tenth Amendment was intended to resolve uncertainties between the national and state governments over delegated and reserved powers. Such uncertainties, according to Marshall, were perpetually "arising, and would continue to arise as long as our system shall exist."[16] The CSA Constitution resolved that issue to the detriment of centralized power.

Article I, Section 2, Clause 1, of the CSA Constitution

Article I, section 2, clause 1, stipulates that the "House of Representatives shall be composed of members chosen every second year by the people of the several States; and the electors in each State shall *be citizens of the Confederate States,* and have the qualifications requisite for electors of the most numerous branch of the State Legislature; *but no person of foreign birth, not a citizen of the Confederate States, shall be allowed to vote for any officer, civil or political, State or Federal"* (emphasis added). This qualification manifests an appreciation of a Southern community distinct from Northern and Western States. The CSA framers anticipated a deluge of immigration from Northern States and abroad as the Confederacy commercially prospered. In an attempt to mitigate the divisive national politics experienced in the old Union, the CSA framers sought to discourage Northern interests located in CSA States from percolating upwards by essentially disenfranchising non-indigenous Southerners. However, as stipulated in Article IV, section 3, "other States may be admitted into this Confederacy by a vote of two-thirds of the whole House of Representatives and two-thirds of the Senate, the Senate voting by States." So non-Southern interests could have a voice in CSA politics, but only as States, and such States could only be admitted by a two-thirds vote, whereas in the US Constitution, admission to the Union requires only a majority vote.

Article I, Section 2, Clause 5

Article I, section 2, clause 5 stipulates that "the House of

Representatives shall choose their Speaker and other officers; and shall have the sole power of impeachment, *except that any judicial or other Federal officer, resident and acting solely within the limits of any State, may be impeached by a vote of two-thirds of both branches of the legislature thereof"* (emphasis added). The CSA Congress could circumvent this state impeachment power by assigning CSA judicial and other federal officers beyond the limits of any one state. But such circumvention was unlikely, given the strong States' rights mindset of the Confederacy. Nevertheless, the provision is a powerful indication that the States were not to be subservient to CSA judges and bureaucrats. For example, CSA district court judges were for all intents and purposes held accountable to the state legislatures, but the two-thirds vote requirement made that accountability juridically stable.

Article I, Section 6, Clause 2

Article I, section 6, clause 2, provides that "the Congress may, by law, grant to the principal officer in each of the executive departments a seat upon the floor of either House, with the privilege of discussing any measures appertaining to his department." This innovation was a move (or more accurately a turn) towards cabinet government, which would enhance dialogue between the two branches of government. Unlike a committee hearing, where executive department heads are questioned by legislators, this arrangement provided the executive branch opportunities to address the Congress on executive-branch terms, while also allowing members of Congress to question officials outside the highly structured committee system.

Article I, Section 7, Clause 2

Article I, section 7, clause 2, provides the CSA president with the line-item veto on appropriation bills. It stipulates: "The President may approve any appropriation and disapprove any other appropriation in the same bill. In such case he shall, in signing the bill, designate the appropriations disapproved; and shall return a copy of such appropriations, with his objections, to the House in which the bill shall have originated; and the same proceedings shall then be had as in case of other bills disapproved by the President." Legislative pork-barrel riders to appropriation bills would be subjected to executive scrutiny and, if vetoed, subjected to a congressional two-thirds vote override.

Article I, Section 8, Clause 1

Article I, section 8, clause 1, stipulates that "the Congress shall have the power to lay and collect taxes, duties, imposts, and excises, *for revenue necessary* to pay the debts, provide for the common defense, *and carry on the Government of the Confederate States; but no bounties shall be granted from the Treasury; nor shall any duties or taxes on importations from foreign nations be laid to promote or foster any branch of industry* [emphasis added]; and all duties, imposts, and excises shall be uniform throughout the Confederate States." Notably absent (also absent in the preamble) is reference to the "general Welfare" as a congressional objective. This provision put to rest the bugbear of US national politics by constitutionally prohibiting protectionism, a tax policy used to benefit Northern industrial over Southern agrarian interests.

Article I, Section 8, Clause 3

Article I, section 8, clause 3, stipulates the congressional power "to regulate commerce with foreign nations, and among the several States, and with Indian tribes; *but neither this, nor any other clause contained in the Constitution, shall ever be construed to delegate the power to Congress to appropriate money for any internal improvement intended to facilitate commerce; except for the purpose of furnishing lights, beacons, and buoys, and other aids to navigation upon the coasts, and the improvement of harbors and the removing of obstructions in river navigation, in all which cases, such duties shall be laid on the navigation facilitated thereby, as may be necessary to pay the costs and expenses thereof*" (emphasis added). This provision is a balanced approach to the regionally divisive internal improvements through which revenues from import duties generated by Southern exports were mostly expended in the North and West. The provision did not prohibit federally funded internal improvements, but based those improvements on a user-pay system (those businesses that benefited from the public expenditures paid for those benefits).

Article I, Section 8, Clause 4

Article I, section 8, clause 4, stipulates the congressional power "to establish uniform *laws* of naturalization, and uniform laws on the subject of bankruptcies, throughout the *Confederate* States; *but no law of Congress shall discharge any debt contracted before the passage of the same*" (emphasis added). The change from uniform "rules" to "laws" shifted the naturalization process to the national government.[17] This mitigated confusion stemming from Article IV's privileges and immunities clause, by standardizing the naturalization process throughout the Confederacy. The bankruptcy provision reassured creditors, within and outside the CSA, that debts would not be discharged due to secession.

Article I, Section 8, Clause 7

Article I, section 8, clause 7, stipulates the congressional power "to establish post-offices and post *routes; but the expenses of the Post-office Department, after the first day of March, in the year of our Lord eighteen hundred and sixty-three, shall be paid out of its own revenue*" (emphasis added). This provision was designed to wean the CSA postal service from governmental subsidies and direct it towards a user-pay system.

Article I, Section 9, Clause 1

Article I, section 9, clause 1, stipulates that "the importation of *negroes of the African race, from any foreign country other than the slaveholding States or Territories of the United States of America, is hereby forbidden; and Congress is required to pass such laws as shall effectually prevent the same*" (emphasis added). This provision was in response to the foreign slave trade, which it bans, and to Northern States that were essentially deporting African-Americans from their jurisdictions, such as Illinois, which had a very active deportation program. Territories were exempted because they were considered to be the property of the CSA. It is notable that the CSA Congress was "required" to ban such trade.

Article I, Section 9, Clause 2

Article I, section 9, clause 2, stipulates that "Congress shall have the power to prohibit the introduction of slaves from any State not a member of, or Territory belonging to, this Confederacy." This provision pertains to slaves from States not part of the CSA. Similar to Article I, section 9, clause 1, of the US Constitution, without the twenty-year period for importing slaves, the CSA Congress was immediately authorized to ban the importation of slaves from non-CSA slave States. For example, if a Southern slave state decided to remain in the Union, slave owners from that state could not sell those slaves in the CSA.

Article I, Section 9, Clause 4

Article I, section 9, clause 4, stipulates that "no bill of attainder, ex post facto law, *law denying or impairing the right of property in negro slaves shall be passed"* (emphasis added). This prohibition applied to the CSA Congress, not to the States. Manumission was a state option. The provision reflects the anticipation that free States would join the Confederacy, so it made it impossible for them to use the national government to impose manumission on slave States.

Article I, Section 9, Clause 6

Article I, section 9, clause 6, stipulates that "no tax or duty shall be laid on articles exported from any State *except by a vote of two-thirds of both Houses"* (emphasis added). Unlike its US counterpart, Article I, section 9, clause 5, which prohibits any export tax or duty, this provision allows for such taxes and duties if approved by a two-thirds congressional vote. Consistent with Article I, section 8, clause 3, duties and taxes on exports were options of the user-pay policy, which held that "such duties shall be laid on the navigation facilitated thereby, as may be necessary to pay the costs and expenses thereof."

Article I, Section 9, Clause 9

Article I, section 9, clause 9, stipulates that "Congress shall appropriate no money from the Treasury, except by a vote of two-thirds of both Houses, taken by nays and yeas, unless it be asked and estimated by some one of the heads of departments, and submitted to Congress by the president; or for the purpose of paying its own expenses and contingencies; or for the payment of claims against the Confederate States, the justice of which shall have been judicially declared by a tribunal for the investigation of claims against the Government, which it is hereby made the duty of Congress to establish." These innovations were designed to impose fiscal responsibility on the CSA government and to avoid the inefficiencies and abuses of its US counterpart. Pork-barrel legislative politics required a two-thirds vote, unless introduced by the executive branch. The executive branch was constitutionally responsible for budgeting and accounting, serving as a brake on regionally based legislative coalitions seeking to maximize their influence over budgeting.[18] Distrust of legislative politics is manifested in a new tribunal to be created by the CSA Congress. Anticipating US claims against the CSA stemming from secession, determining the dollar amounts of claims was taken outside the legislative process and made the responsibility of a CSA tribunal to investigate, adjudicate, and determine the settlement amounts.

Article I, Section 9, Clause 10

Article I, section 9, clause 10, stipulates that "bills appropriating money shall specify, in Federal currency, the exact amount of each appropriation, and the purpose for which it is made; and Congress shall grant no extra compensation to any public contractor, officer, agent, or servant, after such contract has been made or such service rendered." This provision effectively prohibits cost overruns, thereby enhancing the credibility of the negotiating process for government contracts.

Article I, Section 9, Clause 20

Article I, section 9, clause 20, stipulates that "every law, or resolution having the force of law, shall relate to but one subject, and that shall be expressed in the title." This provision restricted the use of omnibus bills, thereby requiring that each bill legislatively stand or fall on its own merits.

Article I, Section 10, Clause 3

Article I, section 10, clause 3, stipulates: "No State shall, without the consent of Congress, lay any duty *on tonnage, except on sea-going vessels for the improvement of its rivers and harbors navigated by the said vessels; but such duties shall not conflict with any treaties of the Confederate States with foreign nations. And any surplus revenue thus derived shall, after making such improvement, be paid to the common Treasury. . . . But when any river divides or flows through two or more States, they may enter into compacts with each other to improve the navigation thereof*" (emphasis added). This provision empowered the States by permitting them, without the consent of Congress, to place duties on seagoing vessels, the proceeds of which were to be used to improve river transportation and harbors.[19] Moreover, States connected by a river could also enter into compacts to improve navigation. This complements the Confederacy's commitment to free trade (i.e., surplus revenue was to be paid into the Confederate treasury, thereby guarding against the practice of using duties to promote unrelated internal improvements and protectionism) within the context of a user-pay system.

Article II, Section 1

Article II, section 1, stipulates: "The Executive power shall be vested in a President of the *Confederate* States of America. *He and the Vice President shall hold their offices fo*r the term of *six* years; *but the President shall not be reeligible*" (emphasis added). With the limitation to one six-year term, the hope was to elevate the statesmanship of the CSA president, while limiting the opportunities for patronage.[20]

Article II, Section 2, Clause 3

Article II, section 2, clause 3, stipulates: "The principal officer in each of the executive departments, and all persons connected with the diplomatic service, may be removed from office at the pleasure of the President. All other civil officers of the executive department may be removed by the President at any time, or other appointing power, when their services are unnecessary, or for dishonesty, incapacity, inefficiency, misconduct, or neglect of duty; and, when so removed, the removal shall be reported to the Senate, together with the reasons therefor." By serving at the pleasure of the president, those executive department officials would be more accountable to the president, and less accountable to congressional committees and/or interest groups with agendas working against the president's policy agenda.[21]

Article II, Section 2, Clause 4

Article II, section 2, clause 4, stipulates that "the President shall have the power to fill up vacancies that may happen during the recess of the Senate, by granting commissions which shall expire at the end of their next session. *But no person rejected by the Senate shall be reappointed to the same during their ensuing recess*" (emphasis added). This provision strengthened the confirmation hand of the Senate, especially in light of the fact that at the time Senate recesses would stretch for months, not weeks.

Article III, Section 2

Article III, section 2, stipulates that "the judicial power shall extend to all cases arising under this Constitution, the laws of the *Confederate* States, and treaties made, or which shall be made, under their authority; to all cases affecting ambassadors, other public ministers and consuls; to all cases of admiralty and maritime jurisdiction; to controversies to which the *Confederate* States shall be a party; to controversies between two or more States; between a State and citizens of another State, *where the State is plaintiff;* between citizens claiming lands under grants of different States; and between a State or the citizens thereof, and foreign states, citizens, or subjects; *but no State shall be sued by a citizen or subject of any foreign state"* (emphasis added). The CSA framers incorporated the US Constitution's Eleventh Amendment sovereign immunity protection into Article III, thereby prohibiting a state from being sued in CSA courts by individuals without the state's consent.

Article IV, Section 2, Clause 1

Article IV, section 2, clause 1, stipulates that "the citizens of each State shall be entitled to all the privileges and immunities of citizens in the several States, *and shall have the right of transit and sojourn in any State of this Confederacy, with their slaves and other property; and the right of property in said slaves shall not be thereby impaired"* (emphasis added). This provision not only incorporated the Dred Scott ruling that slave property throughout the CSA was constitutionally protected, but, perhaps more importantly, also acknowledged that free States would be members of the CSA.

Article IV, Section 3, Clause 1

Article IV, section 3, clause 1, stipulates that "other States may be admitted into this Confederacy by a vote of two-thirds of the whole House of Representatives and two-thirds of the Senate, the Senate voting by States." Expansion of the CSA was not only anticipated, but encouraged. But unlike the US Constitution, which required only a majority vote, the two-thirds vote required by the CSA facilitated greater consensus within the CSA regarding the rate and character of expansion.

Article IV, Section 3, Clause 3

Article IV, section 3, clause 3, stipulates: "The Confederate States may acquire new territory; and Congress shall have the power to legislate and provide governments for the inhabitants of all territory belonging to the Confederate States, lying without the limits of the several States; and may permit them, at such times, and in such manner, as it may by law provide, to form States to be admitted into the Confederacy. In all such territory, the institution of negro slavery, as it now exists in the Confederate States, shall be recognized and protected by Congress and by the territorial government; and the inhabitants of the several Confederate States and Territories shall have the right to take to such Territory any slaves lawfully held by them in any of the States or Territories of the Confederate States." This provision resolved the territorial crisis that had plagued the US. Consistent with the US Supreme Court's Dred Scott ruling, the provision, as is the case with clause 1 of sections 2 and 3 of this article, does not require slavery as a constitutional prerequisite for admission into the CSA. And as discussed later in this book, the fate of slavery was left to the States, as was the case under the US Constitution, through which manumission was effected in a majority of the States.

Article V, Section 1, Clause 1

Article V, section 1, clause 1, stipulates: *"Upon the demand of any three States, legally assembled in their several conventions, the Congress shall summon a Convention of all the States, to take into consideration such amendments to the Constitution as the said States shall concur in suggesting at the time when the said demand is made; and should any of the proposed amendments to the Constitution be agreed on by the said Convention—voting by States—and the same be ratified by the Legislatures of two-thirds of the several States, or by conventions in two-thirds thereof*—as one or the other mode of ratification may be proposed by the *general Convention—they shall thence forward form a part of this Constitution.* But no State shall, without its consent, be deprived of its equal *representation* in the Senate" (emphasis added). This provision is designed to protect the interests of a minority of States from being victimized by a majority of States. Three States could tie up the national government by repeatedly convening constitutional conventions to redress their grievances. Moreover its US Article V counterpart requires a two-thirds majority of the Congress or a national convention called by two-thirds of the States to propose and three-fourths of either state legislatures or conventions to ratify proposed amendments, the CSA Constitution requires only two-thirds of all the States to ratify. This CSA constitutional innovation is the most substantial, and deserves further elaboration.[22]

⊀ II ⊁

The CSA amendment process stems from the Confederate compact-covenant ideal, in which States' rights were not a hurdle to overcome, but a principle to be constitutionally protected. Defending that principle is defending democracy. The issue with the States' rights principle, then and now, is that it is too democratic and therefore presents the most serious challenge to the policy objectives of national elites.[23] This issue is as old as the Union. The argument of Publius (the pseudonym used by the authors of *The Federalist Papers*) for ratification of the 1787 Constitution hinged on "his" critique of overbearing state majorities, i.e., too much democracy in the States. The States of the CSA considered the old Union to be a compact among the States, and not a social contract among Americans merely expressing their political will through their respective state conventions. The titles of the ordinances of secession reaffirmed the Confederacy's compact-covenant ideal. South Carolina set the standard: *An Ordinance to Dissolve the Union between the State of South Carolina and the Other States United with her under the Compact Entitled "The Constitution of the United States of America."*[24]

The CSA framers decided to remove ambiguity about how the States of the CSA were tied together. For example, the CSA preamble affirms each state's "sovereign and independent character, in order to form a permanent federal government," in contradistinction to the US Constitution's "more perfect Union." Excluding the US Constitution preamble's "general Welfare" reference removed another hook upon which to hang consolidation aspirations. As instructed by Calhoun, the CSA framers did not equate union with consolidation: "Having ratified and adopted it [the US Constitution], by mutual agreement, they stand in relation of parties to a constitutional compact; and, of course, it is binding between them as a compact, and not on, or over them, as a constitution . . . the people of the several States, in their sovereign capacity, agreed to unite themselves together, in the closest possible connection that could be formed, without merging their respective sovereignties into one common sovereignty."[25]

This compact theory is articulated in South Carolina's secession declaration: "We maintain that in every compact between two or more parties, the obligation is mutual; that the failure of one of the contracting parties to perform a material part of the agreement, entirely releases the obligation of the other; and that, when no arbiter is provided, each party is remitted to his own judgment to determine the fact of failure, with all its consequences."[26] The parties to the compact were the States, and the Confederate government was their common agent, with each state reserving the prerogative to determine whether there has been a material breach concerning the obligations of the compact and how to remedy any such breach. Remedies included constitutional conventions, nullification, interposition, and, if all else failed, secession.

The Confederate compact theory was well within the American political tradition, as evidenced by the 1798 Kentucky and Virginia Resolutions, written by Thomas Jefferson and James Madison, respectively: "The Government created by this compact (the US Constitution) was not made the exclusive or final judge of the extent of the powers delegated to itself. . . . But in all other cases of compact among parties having no common Judge, each party has an equal right to judge for itself, as well of infractions as the mode and measure of redress."[27]

The CSA's amendment process is a procedural mechanism designed to maintain the compact nature of the CSA Constitution and is a modified version of Calhoun's concurrent majority. The concurrent majority is a constitutional mechanism designed to facilitate compromise, maximize the consent of the governed, and preserve the consensual union of States. Providing the States with the constitutional means to resist usurpations of the central government could (and assuredly would as the union became increasingly economically, socially, and culturally heterogeneous) substantially limit the policy prerogatives of the central government. Such was the intention of the framers of 1787 and 1861; they placed a much greater value on the consent of the governed than on a central government imposing its will. According to Calhoun, "the more extensive and populous the country, the more diversified the condition and pursuits of its population; the richer, the more luxurious, and dissimilar the people, the more difficult it is to equalize the action of the government, and the more easy for one portion of the community to pervert its powers to oppress and plunder the other."[28]

Even though the prospects for "plunder" under the CSA Constitution, with its augmented internal checks and balances on the central government, were much lower, the CSA framers were very cognizant of the building momentum towards centralization once a central government is established. As experience and Calhoun instructed, a dominant national political party will eventually emerge, making constitutional checks and balances nugatory, unless States' rights were procedurally and constitutionally guaranteed. Calhoun stated, "A written constitution certainly has many considerable advantages, but it is a great mistake to suppose that the mere insertion of provisions to restrict and limit the powers of the government, without investing those for whose protection they are inserted with the means of enforcing their observance, will be sufficient to prevent the major and dominant party from abusing its powers. Being the party in the possession of the [central] government, they will, from the same constitution of man which makes government necessary to protect society, be in favor of the powers granted by the constitution and opposed to the restrictions intended to limit them."[29] The emergence of the national two-party system overwhelmed the US Constitution's internal checks and balances. Centralized political power in the hands of a national party is incompatible with the checks and balances designed to preserve a decentralized federal system.

The election of Lincoln personified the trend of national centralization. As a reaction, some of the Southern States (South Carolina, Florida, Mississippi, Louisiana, Alabama, Georgia, and Texas) resorted to the ultimate exercise of States' rights, secession from the Union, as the only effective way to secure their regional minority interests from the hostile policy objectives of the sectional Republican Party. Other Southern States (Virginia, North Carolina, Tennessee, Kentucky, and Arkansas) took a wait and see attitude, eventually siding with the States forming the CSA when they determined that Lincoln's Republican Party was determined to use coercive means to secure a centralized national system of government, a system incompatible with the compact theory of the Union.

In his first inaugural address, President Lincoln rejected the compact theory of the Constitution and reproached the seceded States. He maintained that "no State, upon its own mere motion, can lawfully get out of the Union; that resolves and ordinances to that effect, are legally void; and that acts of violence within any State or States against the authority of the United States, are insurrectionary or revolutionary, according to the circumstances."[30] One 1860 pamphlet had stated the South's position:

> The whole question is whether or not the State can release her citizens from their obligations to the federal authority, and protect them under the sufficient shield of her own sovereign authority! . . . Hapless would be the condition of these States if their only alternative lay between submission to a government of self-construed, or, in other words, unlimited powers, and the certainty of coercion, in the case of withdrawal, by force of arms. The way of escape from both extremes is the acknowledged *right of secession*"[31] (emphasis added).

The compact theory underpinning the CSA Constitution was bolstered by its covenantal qualities. Although the States were consensually united within the CSA, it was more of a brotherhood based upon the good faith[32] of the parties than an expedient association for mutual exploitation. In this context, "a covenant differs from a compact in that its moral dimensions take precedence over its legal dimensions."[33] In a covenant, a higher moral force, usually God, is either a party or sponsor of a relationship. In a compact, a higher moral force is not directly involved. Therefore, a compact, though still ethical, depends more on legal grounds for its politics.

The original US Constitution was most certainly a compact document with a strong covenant component. But the constitution adhered to by President Lincoln was a secular legal contract, from which no state "can lawfully get out of." Lincoln's view is what so alarmed Southerners. If strictly a legal document, the US Constitution was amenable to the malice and dishonesty of the Republican Party, twisting its terms to defraud the Southern States when opportunities to do so arose. Coercion displaced good faith as the primary force keeping the Union intact. In the absence of that good faith, there was de facto no covenantal union between the North and South. Secession merely made the separation de jure. Taking confidence in the CSA Constitution's specific reference to the "favor and guidance of Almighty God," Thomas R. R. Cobb "acknowledged the overruling providence of God" as the guarantor of the good faith of the parties to the CSA Constitution.[34]

The three-state minimum to convene a constitutional convention would, in a union of bickering antagonistic States, probably be regularly resorted to and utilized as a council of revision superseding the normal checks and balances. But when considered within the context of the CSA, a context of state sovereignty and the good faith of the parties, the streamlined amendment process was a constitutional mechanism at the disposal of the States to update and/or clarify the terms of their association. For example, what would have been the effect of this amendment process under the US Constitution when the US Supreme Court issued rulings objectionable to several States, or the US Congress passed fiscal policies detrimental to a number of States? A state or States would have the constitutional means to address such matters in a convention of the States and propose remedies. If remedies were not forthcoming, and a pattern of clashing irreconcilable interests becomes the rule rather than the exception, then the States could reevaluate the purpose of their association and act accordingly. The CSA's streamlined amendment process may not necessarily be an efficient way to advance and expand a central government, but the consent of the governed, not governmental growth, was the primary objective of the CSA framers.

Furthermore, a limited central government commensurately reduces the potential for political conflict between the States. Calhoun articulated the Confederate view: "The moment Government is put into operation, as soon as it begins to collect taxes, and make appropriations, the different portions of the community, must, of necessity, bear different and opposing relations in reference to the action of the Government. There must inevitably spring up two interests—a directing and stockholding interest; and interest profiting by the action of the Government, and interested in increasing its powers and action; and another at whose expense the political machine is kept in motion."[35] There may be dissatisfaction among those seeking to utilize the national government to promote their economic and social agendas, but that dissatisfaction lacked the wherewithal to coercively, e.g., militarily, surmount the obstacles used by those seeking to protect their interests from national policies. Decentralization curtails the central government's capacity to resort to coercion. In the CSA, there would not be national internal improvements, funded by regionally biased tariffs and enforced by Jacksonian force bills. Because the CSA central government lacked both the constitutional prerogatives to legitimatize and the capacity to overcome state resistance to such policies, centralization and its corrupting influence were held in check.

◄ III ►

The normative question of the States' capacity to effectively function in a decentralized setting is an important one. Distrust of the States' capacity for judicious self-government that respects fundamental rights is as old as the US Constitution. This is why, in the first Congress, James Madison insisted upon applying a national bill of rights to the States. While discussing a bill of rights in the US House, Madison maintained: "I think there is more danger of those [governmental] powers being abused by the State Governments than by the Government of the United States. The same may be said of the other powers they may possess, if not controlled by the general principle, that laws are unconstitutional which infringe upon the rights of the community."[36] This explains the proposed Federalist amendment (which was passed in the House but defeated in the Senate), to be inserted in Article I, section 10: "No State shall violate the equal rights of conscience, or freedom of the press, or trial by jury in criminal cases."[37] Madison articulated the Federalist position in the Virginia ratifying convention; when discussing religious liberty he stated, "It is better that his [Virginian citizen] security be depended upon from the general [national] legislature, than from one particular state. A particular state may concur in one religious project. But the United States abound in such a variety of sects, that it is a strong security against religious persecution; and it is sufficient to authorize a conclusion, that no one sect will ever be able to outnumber or depress the rest."[38]

The Anti-Federalist response to national supremacy in the areas of political and civil rights was voiced by Rep. Thomas Tudor Tucker: "It seemed to him [Tucker] as if there was a strong propensity in this Government to take upon themselves the guidance of the State Governments, which to his mind implied a doubt of their capacity to govern themselves, and deserved more to be trusted than this did, because the right of the citizen was more secure under it."[39]

Taking the Anti-Federalists' side of the argument, the CSA framers did trust state governments over the national government to judiciously govern, respectful of fundamental rights. This is reflected in their rewrite of the Ninth Amendment to the US Constitution and its location in the CSA Constitution:

US Ninth Amendment: The enumeration in the Constitution, of certain rights, shall not be construed to deny or disparage others retained by the people.

CSA Article VI, clause 5: The enumeration, in the Constitution, of certain rights, shall not be construed to deny or disparage others retained by the people *of the several States* [emphasis added].

Rights "retained by the people" is general and has been distorted to mean a general standard of rights applicable to the national community, whereas rights "retained by the people of the several States" is particular and denotes a diversity of standards to be established by the political processes in the respective States.

The state political processes were augmented by the CSA Constitution's reserved powers clause:

> US Tenth Amendment: The powers not delegated to the United States by the Constitution, nor prohibited by it to the States, are reserved to the States respectively, or to the people.

> CSA Article VI, clause 6: The Powers not delegated to the Confederate States by the Constitution, nor prohibited by it to the States, are reserved to the States, respectively, or to the people *thereof* [emphasis added].

The inclusion of "thereof" clarifies that the American people, the States notwithstanding, have no reserved powers. The reserved powers are reserved to the States and to the people thereof. In other words, the people within the State still reserved certain powers, with the exercise of those powers not contingent upon the approval of the political branches of the national government exercising the reserved powers of the American people. Outside the States there are no reserved powers, neither in the US territories, nor in the District of Columbia, nor in the American people.

The constitutional mandates to apply the CSA bill of rights to the CSA central government and the reserved powers being the exclusive prerogative of the States are reinforced by their placement in Article I, section 9. Counterparts to the US Constitution's first eight amendments were incorporated into the ninth section of Article I. In short, the CSA Constitution restricts the CSA government much more extensively than the US Constitution restricts the US government. In the aftermath of over half a century of wrangling over the status of the States vis-à-vis the US government, the CSA framers placed the CSA government firmly under the heels of the States.

The CSA Constitution moved towards the constitutional resolution of the political monster that tormented the Union, the *imperium in imperio*. There was much less ambiguity about divided sovereignty in the CSA; it remained where it originated, in the States. While sovereignty resided with the people in their respective States, and collectively in the national community when the States acted in unison, the CSA national government was the agent of the States and the state governments the agents of their respective citizens. If national policies were permitted to prevail over the vehement objections of a state, then the citizens of that state would cease to be self-governing regarding those national policies. Under the CSA model of federalism, a state legislature, with a two-thirds vote, could impeach "any judicial or other Federal officer, resident and acting solely within the limits of any State,"[40] convene a constitutional convention with two other States,[41] and, if that fails, secede with the options to remain independent or to accede back into the Confederacy under new arrangements. This is a system of government of, by, and for the people within their respective States, with secession as a state's ultimate weapon against the central government.

A state's right to secede was implicit in both the US and CSA constitutions. The CSA framers concluded that to make that right explicit in the CSA Constitution would be yielding to the Republican party's position that if such a right is not expressly granted, it does not constitutionally exist. Southerners maintained that it is a reserved right of the compact and acknowledged in the law of nations. But the CSA framers were also realists. The seven States that had initially seceded from the Union had the practical problem of attracting the support of the Border States and certain European powers. To explicitly stipulate the right of secession would give the appearance of disparate States temporarily associated under a feeble central government. In reference to the US Constitution, Jefferson Davis contended:

> The simple truth is, that it would have been a very extraordinary thing to incorporate into the Constitution any express provision for the secession of the States and the dissolution of the Union. Its founders undoubtedly desired and hoped that it would be perpetual; against the proposition for power to coerce a State, the argument was that it would be a means, not of preserving, but of destroying the Union. It was not for them to make arrangements for its termination—a calamity which there was no occasion to provide for in advance. . . . It was not necessary in the Constitution to affirm the right of secession, because it was an attribute of sovereignty, and the States had reserved all they had not delegated.[42]

There was no need for the CSA framers to explicitly insert a right of secession. By explicitly recognizing the "sovereign and independent character" of the States in acceding to join the CSA, it was implicit that secession was a reserved power. St. George Tucker[43] stated what was obvious to the framers of the US and CSA constitutions: "The powers delegated to the federal government being all positive, and enumerated according to the ordinary rules of construction, whatever is not enumerated is retained; for *expressum facit tacere tacitum* [that which is expressed makes that which is implied to cease] is a maxim in all cases of construction: it is likewise a maxim of political law, that sovereign states cannot be deprived of any of their rights by implication; nor in any manner whatever by their own voluntary consent, or by submission to a conqueror."[44] Moreover, by substantially augmenting the constitutional constraints on the CSA government, even if the CSA government desired to coercively maintain the CSA as a state or States exercised their constitutional prerogative to secede, it lacked the political and military means to effect such a policy. Under the CSA model, the central government was much more effectively confined behind the walls of States' rights.

✨ IV ✨

In conclusion, to appreciate some probable policy implications of the CSA Constitution, consider those US Supreme Court policies that, in the absence of the States' acquiescence, are precluded under the CSA model: (a) an expansive interpretation of congressional commerce powers,[45] (b) national judicial supremacy,[46] (c) militarily coerced membership in the Union,[47] (d) the supremacy of US treaties and international agreements over the States' Tenth Amendment reserved powers,[48] (e) presidential imperial powers,[49] (f) incremental secularization of the States,[50] (g) an electorally entrenched US Congress,[51] (h) due process privacy rights of abortion, sexuality, etc.[52] The CSA model does not preclude the States from individually adopting and/or rejecting these and other policies within their respective jurisdictions. States' rights is amenable to policy differences among the States. But it does preclude such policies from being imposed upon an unwilling and, for that matter, indifferent, State. For a state government to act it must have the tacit or active consent of its citizenry; it cannot thwart that consent by acting through the national government and/or acquiesce to national policies the people of the State reject. This is well armed States' rights republicanism in contrast to a government under the control of faceless centralized elites.

Chapter II

CONFEDERATE JUSTICE

Considerations of expediency and policy cannot be permitted to control our judgment. We must expound the constitution according to what appears to be its true meaning; and if it be clear that no power to pass the acts in question has been conferred by it, we are bound to declare them void and of no effect, however disastrous may be the consequences of our decision.

Burroughs v. Peyton,
Supreme Court of Virginia, 1864

❧ I ❧

An abstraction frequently referred to, but seldom understood, is the rule of law. One problem is confusing the "rule *of* law" with the "rule *by* law." The distinction is important. For example, as Brian Z. Tamanaha recently wrote, "[Communist] Chinese leaders want rule by law, not rule of law. . . . The difference . . . is that under the rule of law, the law is preeminent and can serve as a check against the abuse of power. Under the rule by law the law can serve as a mere tool for a government that suppresses in a legalistic fashion."[1] The same can be said about the US, as it utilized the rule by law to suppress the CSA. The CSA, on the other hand, consistently upheld the rule of law as the adhesive of the Confederacy, as is evident when the concepts are properly understood.

According to Prof. F. A. Hayek, the rule of law "means that government in all its actions is bound by rules fixed and announced beforehand—rules which make it possible to foresee with fair certainty how the authority will use its coercive powers in given circumstances."[2] Hayek's definition includes fixed rules, government, and those subject to governmental authority. The relationship between a government and the governed, determined by the fixed rules, could include both totalitarian and democratic forms of government. As outlined by Prof. A. V. Dicey, a relationship between the government and the governed, in conformity with the rule of law as understood by English and American standards, requires five interrelated conditions, all of which were present in the CSA.

First, *supremacy of the law* over governmental and nongovernmental persons is controlling. Citizens and governments are subject to the same established laws. Individuals have an area of autonomy within which their rights and duties are secured by pre-established laws.

Second, there is a commitment to an *interpersonal concept of justice,* in which procedural due process is between individuals and not groups. Individuals do and suffer harm, and justice consists in upholding what is right between persons, not between groups.

Third, *governmental discretion* to alter the law cannot be exercised in such a way as to negatively impact the rights and duties of individuals. Arbitrary governmental discretion undermines justice because it makes vulnerable the legal rights of individuals.

Fourth, a *doctrine of judicial precedent* is implemented through a system of superior and inferior courts. Judicial adherence to precedent promotes the stability and predictability in law needed for the exercise of individual rights.

Fifth, *common law* is the substance of judicial precedent. The community values the accumulated wisdom embodied in common law, to the extent that policies that deviate from that wisdom are subject to judicial prohibition.[3]

Because of federalism, the American rule of law is not a unified system of law, but rather systems of law. It is more accurate to write in terms of the American *rules* of law, thereby capturing the diverse legal cultures and systems of the various colonial, state, and national jurisdictions that were and are extant. Diversity among the various jurisdictions (national, state, and territorial) necessarily exists. But within that diversity, Hayek's "fixed rules" and Dicey's interrelated conditions are essential to a proper understanding of the CSA's framers' justification for secession and the formation of the CSA.[4] However, the American rule of law rests upon two important components only hinted at by Professors Hayek and Dicey: first, the making of law in accordance with established procedures, i.e., checks and balances and separation of powers; and second, that the established procedures for making laws must conform to a federal system of popular control and consent.

These components are closely related, but distinct. The second could be described as additional means through which potentially arbitrary governmental actions, under the guise of law, are mitigated. The American rule of law was particularly dependent upon this component, and the CSA Constitution reinforced it.

Of course, any rule of law is purposeful; that is, necessity was and is the supreme lawmaker. For example, superficially the Soviet rule of law was supposedly geared towards a workers' paradise with all sorts of fundamental rights guaranteed. In reality it facilitated the dictatorship of the Communist Party, with heavy reliance on oppressive force and little toleration for individual rights not consistent with the Communist Party's ideology and policy objectives. Even though the Soviet Constitution paid unabashed lip service to the fundamental rights of the Soviet people, those rights were subservient to the Communist Party's primary objective, i.e., perpetuating the party's survival.

It stands to reason that in a free society the linkages between law and consent would be substantial, and that compliance with the law, on balance, would not be oppressive because the laws were by and large self-imposed. In a free society, fundamental individual rights are to be taken seriously; otherwise, the individuals who comprise the free society would be supporting their self-destruction. It also stands to reason that the most highly prized right in a free society is the genuine right of self-government, so that individuals and the communities in which they live are protected against oppressive government.

Within the context of the American rule of law, the preservation of life, liberty, and property was the overarching objective, not a political party in pursuit of an indestructible, powerful union or, as was the case in the former USSR, a workers' super-state paradise. Accordingly, the notion that the "union must be preserved at all costs" is anathema to the rule of law, because it places the preservation of the union as the primary objective, rather than the consent of the governed. Instead of the rule of law being subordinated to the preservation of a coercive union, the union should be subservient to the rule of law. If the union, i.e., the governmental apparatus of centralized policy making, becomes destructive of the rule of law that is grounded in the consent

of the governed, then the union must be either reformed or, if refor-
mation is unlikely, dissolved.

By 1860, Southerners had concluded that reforming the Union
while remaining members in it was unlikely. They proceeded with
what in their minds was their only viable option: dissolving their participation with Northern States in the corrupted old Union. If the
Southern States were to secure the rule of law grounded in the consent
of Southerners within their respective States, they had to reorganize
under a new union. The catalyst for secession was the election of Mr.
Lincoln, an openly sectional politician catapulted into the presidency
by hostile and combative Northern interests. Rather than risk being
arbitrarily subjected to the rule by law of these interests, the Southern
States opted for secession and the rule of law properly understood.

Whereas the Confederates were committed to the rule of law, as
manifested in their acts of secession, the Lincoln Republicans were
radicals who resorted to the ancient custom of force in their drive to
preserve the Union, i.e., their sectional interests, at all costs. The
Lincoln Republicans' treatment of the Southern States leads one to
recall Publius's admonition that "it seems to have been reserved to the
people of this country, by their conduct and example, to decide the
important question, whether societies of men are really capable or not
of establishing good government from reflection and choice, or
whether they are forever destined to depend for their political constitutions on accident and force."[5] There is no question that the CSA was
formed through reflection and choice, whereas Lincoln's Union was a
product of military force.

The Confederates appreciated the importance of reflection and
choice. They also realized that the right to be self-governing and the
rule of law precariously evolved over the centuries. They were not
inclined, as were their Republican counterparts, to dispense with the
rule of law to preserve the CSA, because they viewed the two as inextricably linked. For them, the English common law tradition chronicles
the right to be self-governing in matters great and small, matters of the
nobleman, the citizen, the shopkeeper, and eventually the serf. They
were trained in that common law tradition and acted accordingly.

For example, chapter 39 of the Magna Charta, which stipulates that
"no free man shall be taken or imprisoned or dispossessed, or outlawed,

or banished, or in any way destroyed, nor will we go upon him, nor send upon him, except by the legal judgment of his peers or by the law of the land," and chapter 12, which stipulates that "no scutage or aid shall be imposed in our kingdom except by the common council of the kingdom," are *due process* and no taxation *without representation,* respectively, in embryonic form. Over the centuries, both traditions evolved and were prominent in CSA political and legal culture. Neither was concocted by philosophers and then zealously implemented by radical parties. When the barons at Runnymede forced this and other concessions from King John in 1215, their objective was to constrain arbitrary government, in this case royal absolutism. As significant as the Magna Charta was in the development of English common law, it did not simply spring from the civil war between King John and his barons. Preceding the events at Runnymede, King Henry II constrained his successors by initiating a system of justice that included the use of juries, itinerant justices, and sworn inquests. In 1215, King John capitulated to a rule of law that had been gaining momentum since the beginning of King Henry II's reign in 1154.[6]

The complex story of English common law is one of arbitrariness versus fixed standards. As Tamanaha wrote, the "rule of law congealed into existence in a slow and unplanned manner that commenced in the Middle Ages, with no single source or starting point."[7] Whether the dispute was one of king versus barons or creditor versus debtor, common law sought to apply fixed standards in determining the rights and obligations of the contending parties.

English common law embodies many Runnymedes, where arbitrary government was forced to bow to an established rule of law. However, it would be naïve to assume that the rule of law has always carried the field. English history is replete with the wreckage of the rights and liberties of English subjects compromised by arbitrary governmental action. Nevertheless, the rule of law as embodied in English common law, although not omnipotent, was omnipresent, qualifying and impacting the exercise of political power. Moreover, its impact was recorded in the thousands of cases adjudicated in courts over the centuries, leaving a complicated record of its successes and failures. It was English courts and not simply a parliament that sustained the English rule of law through the centuries.

US and CSA courts played similar roles in those two countries. Courts in the CSA would have continued to do so had they not been disrupted by Union armies and Lincoln's oppressive rule *by* law. Moreover, it is quite plausible that the CSA and state courts would have more humanely dealt with the slavery issue than did Lincoln's opportunistic Emancipation Proclamation.

As the common law record manifests, the rule of law has survived, if not always in fact then at least in principle, and even in principle the wielders of arbitrary power had to contend with its influence.[8] Americans were particularly receptive to English common law and its benefits, as is evidenced in the earliest colonial charters and state constitutions, and the fact that Blackstone's *Commentaries* was the source for legal education and training in America during the most formative period of its development.[9] It was primarily Blackstone, not John Locke and other philosophers, who influenced American political and constitutional development. Rights did not sprout from a mythical Lockean social contract, but evolved over the centuries and were discernible in English and American common law traditions.

Although Americans inherited their legal system from England, there were substantial modifications made to accommodate American circumstances, resulting not in a national system of law but in state-based systems of law. The state nuances were to a significant extent inescapable, due to the cultural variety and autonomy States had in setting and implementing their respective public-policy agendas. As was the case with English common law, the States' legal cultures developed over time and were inherently resistant to sudden change: "No rule of law was ever successful or ever endured unless it received practical general acceptance among the whole body of the people, for the simple reason that universal human experience has demonstrated that a rule of law not accepted by any considerable portion of the people can never be enforced."[10]

The twin pillars of English common law, chapters 12 and 39, in American political and legal development reveal much about the American commitment, both Southern and Northern, to the rule of law. Such being the case, using the underlying principles of chapters 12 and 39, an analysis of CSA judicial politics and jurisprudence reveals a great deal about the system of government to which the

Confederates were committed. What becomes clear is that the regional exceptionalism for which the South is well known includes the South's commitment to a decentralized rule of law, a decentralization that is needed for law to be democratically based upon popular control and consent. A highly centralized court structure charged with determining the rule of law was unacceptable to the Confederates, because such a system was too accommodating towards centralized arbitrary power and therefore too potentially incompatible with the fixed standards inherent in the rule of law.

Is it to be imagined that prior to secession Southern legal traditions were substantially "un-American" or that following secession the Southern States jettisoned their American legal traditions?[11] Were the five interrelated conditions for the rule of law (supremacy of the law, an interpersonal concept of justice, the absence of arbitrary governmental discretion, adherence to the doctrine of judicial precedence, and high regard for common law) widely present and practiced in the Southern courts in 1860 but forgotten in 1861? Not only were those conditions present throughout, but the vigor of their presence under wartime circumstances is convincing evidence of Southerners' commitment to the rule of law.

The circumstantial chaos of the Confederacy's brief but vibrant existence is worth notice. Not only were Southerners confronted with the daunting task of establishing a new central government, but they were compelled to do so while preparing to fight a war of apocalyptic proportions, a war that they well knew would be for their political independence. They were very cognizant that their destiny would not be stagnant, but evolutionary. Their organic view of Southern social institutions and the Southern economic system necessitated an openness towards change to meet the challenges that the nineteenth century presented. At heart conservative, Southerners valued stability over change, but they were also realists and accepted change as inevitable. For example, noting the changes that had occurred between 1832 and 1853, one Virginian novelist, John Pendleton Kennedy, remarked:

> The old states, especially, are losing their original distinctive habits and modes of life. . . . A traveller may detect but few sectional or provincial varieties in the general observances and customs of society, and the

pride, or rather the vanity, of the present day is leading us into a very notable assimilation with foreign usages. . . . The fruitfulness of modern invention in the arts of life, the general fusion of thought through the medium of an extra-territorial literature, which from its easy domestication among us is scarcely regarded as foreign, the conveniences and comfort of European customs which have been incorporated into our scheme of living—all these aided and diffused by our extraordinary facilities of travel and circulation, have made sad work, even in the present generation, with those old *nationalisms* that were so agreeable to the contemplation of an admirer of the picturesque in character and manners.[12]

The trickles of changes observed by Kennedy would become torrents by 1861. Southern independence brought with it profound changes in the economic and social landscapes of the South. One thing is certain: within the context of social, economic, and political flux, Southerners despised both anarchy and tyranny. In order to steer a course between these two extremes as the Southern United States became the Confederate States of America, Southerners found both comfort and guidance in the rule of law, the stabilizing principles of which are the fundamental rights of life, liberty, and property.

Following a well-worn path of conflict resolution inherent in common law, Southerners found solace in their courts, which protected fundamental rights from actual and potential violations. As was the case in the antebellum South, the judiciary provided the framework in which fundamental rights found refuge during the war.

Nevertheless, prevailing scholarship persists in denigrating the Confederacy in an attempt to raise Mr. Lincoln's policies above criticism. Lincoln, in other words, had to save Southerners from themselves. One such scholar maintains:

The traditional view of civil liberties in the Confederacy remains dangerously untested by documentary research. . . . But public policy and administrative practice diverged sharply in the Confederacy, and liberty was more severely restricted for longer periods and over larger areas than mere legislative history suggests. . . . In the case of the Confederacy, it appears that modernization went hand in hand with proscription of civil liberty.[13]

Why is it "dangerous" almost 150 years after Appomattox? Presumably, to equate the CSA with the maintenance of the rule of law is to tarnish the justification for Lincoln's war and the centralized, indissoluble Union it produced. This explains why the prevailing pro-Lincoln "documentary research" is highly selective and uses straw men from which to draw conclusions about the CSA as a whole. Conclusions such as the CSA's reliance on "political repression" of individuals and party oppression against non-Democrats are utilized to portray the CSA as unwilling to take the rule of law seriously.[14]

Is there case-law evidence to refute the charge that Confederate policy substantially deviated from the rule of law and was based upon repression of civil liberties?[15] There is evidence for and against the Confederacy's commitment to the rule of law, just as is the case in the US then and now. No legal system is without instances of procedural and substantive violations of the rule of law. But the preponderance of the evidence shows that, within the context of the forms and procedures of the Confederate legal system, procedural and substantive justice was the norm, not the exception. Being part and parcel of an American civilization very much committed to the rule of law, courts throughout the Confederacy sustained and advanced the rule of law under extremely trying circumstances. The amazing fact about Confederate justice was its predominance under tremendous wartime hardships.

In spite of the political, economic, and social tumult that accompanied events of 1861 to 1865, including military actions in and occupation of the Confederacy by hostile armies, the CSA's record of adherence to the American rule of law bodes very well for how the CSA would have developed had its independence been permanent. It not merely manifests a commitment to the fundamental rights of life, liberty, and property, but reveals inherent contradictions between those commitments and slavery. These contradictions were certain to be adjudicated in Southern state courts to the benefit of fundamental rights. It is highly probable that Southern courts would have been instrumental in facilitating the demise of slavery, had the Confederacy been left alone and its leaders not killed in battle, disenfranchised in postbellum America, and/or financially and emotionally ruined to the point of despair. Indeed, de jure slavery ended in 1865 with the Thirteenth Amendment, but de facto slavery is another matter. The

CSA was much better prepared to deal with both forms of slavery than were the plundering occupation forces of the US Army.

Moreover, centralized power with the capacity to recklessly end slavery has the capacity to enslave not only individuals but entire States. This is not necessarily the slavery of laborers in Southern cotton fields or Soviet gulags, but a more sinister type of slavery, a slavery of the mind and spirit through which regional cultures are swallowed up by the centralized authority and digested into a bland national conformity. Regional distinctiveness is replaced with national uniformity, which in turn feeds into an increasing global uniformity. The destruction of the traditional American rule of law in order to facilitate the integration of local, state, and national courts into a transnational court system will, in large measure, fuel progress towards centralized global uniformity. An analysis of Confederate and state case law is our window through which to view this real but unappreciated tension between the traditional American rule of law and hyper centralization.

The Confederate commitment to the rule of law is especially apparent when the circumstances under which the legal community functioned are considered. For example, even though many judges, lawyers, and court administrators left their public and private positions for military service, the courts were not ignored. To address these and other contingencies, state legislatures passed laws directing the continuances of cases until the cessation of hostilities. And in those instances when CSA and state courts could not function because their jurisdictions fell under Union control, venues and dockets were adjusted to accommodate litigating parties. Courts were operational when and where circumstances permitted, and in those instances when circumstances were not favorable, judges and legislators made reasonable adjustments, always with an eye to preserving the rule of law.[16]

A review of cases tried in those courts that were operating reveals an incredible commitment to the traditional American rule of law. What is notable about these cases is the diversity of opinions, the high quality of the legal arguments, the focus on fundamental rights, and the fact that the decisions commanded the respect and compliance of the executive and legislative branches of government.

The Confederate commitment to keep the courts open and accessible is a phenomenal testimony to the rule of law in a country fighting for its very survival against a very formidable and determined foe. The following case samples are impressive tributes to Confederate justice.

⊀ II ⊁

Impressment is succinctly defined as the "taking of persons or property to aid in the defense of the country, with or without the consent of the persons concerned."[17] Article I, section 9, clause 16, of the CSA Constitution stipulates that "nor shall private property be taken for public use, without just compensation." Settled law defines just compensation as "compensation which is fair to both the owner and the public when property is taken for public use . . . the full monetary equivalent of the property taken."[18] Actual impressment and the determination of just compensation are two distinct processes. Because the CSA operated under the laws and court decisions in effect at the time of secession, its impressment policy was the same as that of the US.

Based upon US Supreme Court precedent established in 1813, a CSA impressment agent's misconduct did not make the government liable for damages. Subordinating property rights to the governmental exegeses, US legal precedent, as articulated by Justice Robert R. Livingston, ruled that "it is better that an individual should now and then suffer by such mistakes, than to introduce a rule against an abuse, of which, by improper collusions, it would be very difficult for the public to protect itself."[19]

Dissatisfied with that US precedent, on March 26, 1863, the CSA Congress passed new legislation to enhance the procedural safeguards of property rights without compromising legitimate military impressment prerogatives.[20] Provisions of the law stipulate:

Whenever the exigencies of any army in the field are such as to make impressments of forage, articles of subsistence, or other property, absolutely necessary, then such impressments may be made by the officer or officers whose duty it is to furnish such forage, articles of subsistence or other property for such army. In cases where the owner of such property and the impressing officers cannot agree upon the value thereof, it shall be the duty of such impressing officer, upon an affidavit in writing of the owner of such property, or his agent, that such property was grown, raised or produced by said owner, or is held or has been purchased by him, not for sale of speculation, but for his own use or consumption, to cause the same to be ascertained and determined by the judgment of two loyal and disinterested citizens of the city, county, or parish in which such impressments may be made; one to be selected by the owner, one by the impressing officer, and in the event of their disagreement, these two shall choose an umpire of like qualifications, whose decision shall be final. The persons thus selected, after taking an oath to appraise the property impressed, fairly and impartially, (which oath, as well as the affidavit provided for in this section, the impressing officer is hereby authorized to administer and certify,) shall proceed to assess just compensation for the property so impressed, whether the absolute ownership, or the temporary use thereof, only is required.[21]

The second section of the statute mandates precise documentation of impressments; the third and fourth sections provided that when appraisements were impracticable, the secretary of war was to comply with sections one and two as soon as practical; the fifth section provided for a Board of Appraisers consisting of two commissioners in each state, with one appointment to be made by the president and one by the governor; the sixth section provided dispute resolution over the "quality of the article or property impressed." And the seventh section prohibited the impressment of "property necessary for the support of the owner and his family." On April 27, 1863, the CSA Congress amended the act by stipulating that if the impressment officers disagree about the appraised evaluation, the disapproval shall be forwarded to the Board of Appraisers in the state where the property is located and to the owner (or his agent or attorney), for a final determination to be made by the former.

These statutory mandates did not preclude court challenges. As state case law makes evident, Southern judges were committed to a rule of law that valued property rights not circumstantially, i.e., for national security, but as an inherent individual right independent of CSA statutes.[22]

Tyson v. Rogers[23]

Harrison Rogers filed suit for a possessory warrant[24] against Capt.

William Tyson, commandant of the CSA military hospitals in Dalton, Georgia, for the impressments of slaves belonging to Rogers and others in the Dalton area. Tyson impressed sixty slaves to work as cooks and nurses, after the soldiers serving in those positions were called for active duty. Georgia Superior Court Judge Walker ordered that the impressed Negroes be returned to their homes, on the grounds that CSA law permitted such impressments only in cases of *extreme necessity,* and the facts of the case did not present a case of extreme necessity.

Georgia Supreme Court Justice Lyon noted that army regulations provided two modes for obtaining cooks and nurses for hospitals: by detail from enlisted men or volunteers, and by hire from outside the army. If after exhausting those two modes hospital nurses and cooks were still urgently needed, then and only then was impressing private property an option. The justice surmised, "I very greatly doubt whether any person, whatever may be his official character, has the right to seize the private property of the citizen, no matter how great may be the public exigency, so long as the law affords protection, unless such seizure be especially authorized by law, and then only upon just compensation made of which the impressing officer, the Government, nor its agents must judge."[25]

Cox & Hill v. Major Cummings[26]

The facts of the case are as follows: Cox & Hill were owners of a warehouse in Atlanta, in possession of 33,942 pounds of brown sugar, contained in thirty-five barrels and owned by Jones & Company of Richmond. The sugar was valued at $1.10 per pound, and the barrels $3.75 each. Major Cummings, a CSA commissary of subsistence, on May 23, 1863, notified the agent of Jones & Company that he would impress the sugar, paying seventy-five cents per pound. Jones & Company's agent declined that price, maintaining that it was well below the market value of the sugar. Jones & Company proceeded to make arrangements to ship the sugar to Richmond, at which time Major Cummings seized the sugar by armed force. In a justice of the peace court, Cox & Hill filed a possessory warrant by which Major Cummings was arrested, the sugar seized, and the major permitted to plead his case. Major Cummings based the legality of the seizure on

the 1863 Act of Congress authorizing impressments. The justices of
the peace ordered him to return the sugar to Cox & Hill and pay the
costs. Major Cummings appealed the decision to the Superior Court of
Fulton County, which reversed the judgments of the justice of the
peace court and raised the price per pound from seventy-five cents to
eighty-five cents. Cox & Hill appealed the Superior Court's judgments
to the Georgia Supreme Court, which reversed the Superior Court's
judgments and decided for the property owners.

In the opinion written by Chief Justice Lumpkin, the issues addressed
by the Supreme Court are threefold: first, what is just compensation as
stipulated in the CSA Constitution; second, how and when is it to be
ascertained; and third, how, when, and in what is it to be paid?

In response to the counsel for the plaintiffs' claim that the right of emi-
nent domain is a reserved power of the States, not a prerogative of the CSA
government, Chief Justice Lumpkin held, "affirming the great principles
of the common law," that "the power to take private property for public
use exists in the Confederate Constitution, and that Congress possesses
this power, with the limitation prescribed—that is, by making just compensation."[27] Just compensation can only be assured if the property owners have meaningful input into determining the value of the property.

Hence, private property can be taken for public use in one of three
ways: "1. By the agreement of the parties, that is, by stipulation
between the agents of the Government and the owner; 2. By commissioners mutually selected by the parties; and 3. By the intervention of
a jury."[28] Citing the US case law (*Vanhorne's Lessee v. Dorrance*), Chief
Justice Lumpkin maintained:

> The interposition of a jury is in such a case a constitutional guard upon
> property, and a necessary check to legislative authority. It is a barrier
> between the Legislature and the individual which ought not to be
> removed. As long as it is preserved, the rights of private property will
> be in no danger of being violated, except in cases of absolute necessity
> or great public utility.[29]

Chief Justice Lumpkin concluded that property owners can be justly
deprived of their property when the public good requires such
deprivations. But any encroachment upon property rights must be

compensated with the fair cash value of the property at the time the property was seized, with compensation paid to the owners in a timely manner. The problem with Major Cummings' actions was that the seized sugar was not valued at a fair cash value. The seized sugar was *choice sugar,* and the commissioners did not determine a fixed price for the higher quality of sugar. Reversing the judgment of the lower court, the Supreme Court remanded the case back to the Superior Court, with instructions for a special jury to determine the just compensation to be paid to the plaintiffs, "unless the parties shall before that time agree upon the price to be paid for the sugar."[30]

Chief Justice Lumpkin's preference for a local jury to determine the fair market price for seized property rankled CSA officials, who contended that local juries preferred local profits over national interests. The chief justice directly addressed that nationalistic bias:

> It is the duty of the Government to provide some fair and proper mode to ascertain the value of property taken, and to pay for it without delay . . . the amount to be assessed by a proper tribunal and paid in money. It is a debt against the public, who takes the property, and must be paid like all other debts. The rule we hold to be this: the fair cash value of the property taken for public use, if the owner were willing to sell and the Government desired to buy, at that time and place and in that form, would be the measure of just compensation. And let not Congress legislate upon the idea that the people are too corrupt to be trusted. For if so, they are unworthy of the boon for which we are fighting, and our martyred heroes have sacrificed their lives in vain.[31]

Four months later, the state court declared provisions of the Impressment Act to be unconstitutional, because of the act's failure to secure just compensation for impressed property. The legal controversy began in June 1863 when H. C. Cunningham, CSA assistant commissary for Georgia, seized parcels of sugar owned by Campbell, Collins, Lewis, and Singleton. Cunningham offered the owners seventy-five cents per pound, whereas the owners valued the sugar's value to be at least $1.00 per pound. Cunningham based this appraisal on a schedule of prices established by commissioners appointed under section 5 of the 1863 CSA Impressment Act. Dissatisfied with the schedule, the owners applied for and obtained possessory warrants from Georgia

Superior Court Judge Lochrane. In September 1863 Judge Lochrane ordered that the sugar be restored to its owners, unless the CSA government assess and pay market price for the sugar, which had increased to $1.25 per pound. The CSA appealed.

Citing both national and state case-law precedents, Georgia Supreme Court Judge Jenkins based the court opinion on five principles. First, there is an inherent power to impress property without the consent of the owner; second, public necessity or utility are preconditions for the impressments of private property; third, impressments must be statutorily authorized by the legislature; fourth, legislative authorization must include provisions for just compensation; and fifth, if provisions for just compensation are not provided for in the statute, the courts may declare the statute to be a nullity.[32]

Counsel for the CSA argued that the impressments were sanctioned by powers inherent in the CSA government, predicated upon higher laws such as *salus populi, suprema lex,* which confer on governments powers to address emergencies of "urgent necessity" to secure the safety of the people. Judge Jenkins acknowledges that there are inherent powers based upon an "unwritten *suprema lex*" so that governments may address cases of "extreme necessity" without which "there is no safety for the people . . . repulsion of an invading army, the stay of pestilence, or the arrest of conflagration—instances usually employed to illustrate the idea of great public necessity."[33] But the impressments under dispute were not due to "extreme necessity inducing and justifying action upon the principle *salus populi, suprema lex.*" These impressments were "authorized by statute, for which conformity to a written Constitution is claimed." Because the impressments were not cases of extreme necessity, but of public utility in order to prevent future shortages of sugar, they must conform to the authorizing statute, which in turn must be sanctioned by the CSA Constitution.[34]

The word *necessity* does not occur in the clause of the Constitution conferring or recognizing the power of impressments. The 16th paragraph, 9th section, 1st article, after providing sundry safeguards to personal rights, concludes thus: *"nor shall private property be taken for public use, without just compensation."* It is not, "nor shall private property be taken *to meet a public necessity, but for public use,* etc.[35]

The CSA Constitution does not sanction the statute under which Cunningham impressed the property, because it did not include a reliable mechanism for arriving at a fair market value at the time of the impressment. The price schedules, established as many as sixty days in advance of impressments, in varying locales, were deemed to be inefficient and arbitrary. Judge Jenkins was determined to protect property rights, limit the confiscatory powers of the national government, and ensure an equitable impressment policy by deferring to market forces. He stipulated: "The impressments authorized by the Constitution, are not designed to cheapen commodities for the Government, but to insure supplies at fair prices. Unless the Government pays prices which citizen consumers pay, the result will be that it levies contributions from one portion of the people in support of the war, from which all others escape. The difference in price paid by the citizen, on purchase, to one dealer, and the price paid by the Government on impressments, to another, will be the measure of contribution unjustly wrested from the latter."[36]

In response to criticisms that state judges were imperiling the survival of the CSA through judicial interference with the necessary war measures of the national government, Judge Jenkins issued a classic statement of judicial responsibility. He claimed:

> Judges as well as legislators are sworn to support the Constitution; and this they are to do in war, as well as in peace. We yield to none in respect for the Congress of the Confederate States; we would at all times, and especially in times like the present, most reluctantly dissent from their construction of the Constitution; we would, in cases of doubtful meaning, incline to give them the benefit of the doubt, for the safety of the country. Beyond this point of concession, not even war, with its attendant horrors, may rightfully impel the judiciary. Positive conviction of constitutional obligation may not be yielded under any circumstances.[37]

Under this strict scrutiny, sections five and six of the 1863 Impressment Act failed the constitutional guarantee that property owners are to be paid market value for impressed property. The practical operation of the statutory sections is not the payment of just compensation to the owners of impressed property, but rather the regulation of prices to the benefit of the government.[38] Thus, the sections are void and the impressment of property under the authority of those sections is illegal.[39]

White v. Ivey and White v. Pease[40]

In March of 1865 the Georgia Supreme Court combined two cases, *White v. Ivey* and *White v. Pease.* Capt. Benjamin F. White was the commandant of the CSA post in Albany and, in October 1864, proceeded to impress the hotel owned by Ivey and the drugstore owned by Pease for use as a hospital. The owners were given three days by the CSA quartermaster to vacate their properties. Ivey and Pease sought and were issued an injunction by the Superior Court restraining the possession of the properties by the CSA Army. The army maintained that the impressments of the buildings were a public necessity due to the proximity of hostile forces and increased casualties; the owners maintained that the impressments were not a public necessity, but designed to more comfortably accommodate the hospital surgeons and their families.

The case was heard and decided by Judge J. Lyons. Based upon a strict construction of the March 26, 1863, CSA Impressment Act, Judge Lyons excluded real property from being impressed by the CSA. The statute states that "whenever the exigencies of any army in the field are such as to make impressments of forage, articles of subsistence, or other property, absolutely necessary, then such impressments may be made."[41] Judge Lyons maintained that if real property was intended to be subjected to impressments, it would have to be authorized by the phrase "other property" noted in the statute. He concluded that such was not the intention of the CSA Congress: "The terms 'other property' were not intended to cover real estate and all other property; but they were used in a much more limited sense, to signify that kind of personal or perishable property answering to that kind of property specified in the act, and absolutely necessary for the army in the field. We arrive at this conclusion, not only from an application of the general expression to this clause, that an enumeration of one class, or grade, of persons or things, followed by such general expressions as this, does not include other persons or things of a different grade, or class, without other and more particular reference thereto, but from a careful consideration of the other parts of the said act."[42] Additionally, the February 16, 1864, amendment of the 1863 Impressment Act requires immediate compensation for the seized property and contains certain exceptions to impressments, such as the seizure of supplies necessary for the support of the property owner and his family. Even if it was the intent of Congress to expand the impressments powers of the army as public necessity required, in order to protect the rights of the citizens the statutory language must specifically authorize those powers: "At all events, this Court must have a plainer expression of an intention to confer such extraordinary powers on an officer, before we could sanction such acts."[43]

Yulee v. Canova[44]

Yulee v. Canova is an impressment case involving the City of Savannah, Georgia, the Florida Railroad Company, the CSA Army, and approximately 50,000 pounds of sugar. In this case the Florida Supreme Court rigorously upheld the inviolability of contracts and property rights. The facts are as follows: Yulee sold 50,000 pounds of sugar to the City of Savannah in July 1863. Yulee was the owner of the sugar plantation that produced the sugar and the railroad company that transported it. While in transit to Savannah the sugar was temporarily stored in a warehouse owned by Yulee.

CSA major Atonia A. Canova proceeded to impress the sugar while in storage. He offered Yulee forty-five cents per pound and warned Yulee that if he refused the offer the sugar would be impressed. Major Canova was informed that the bulk of the sugar had been sold to the City of Savannah. The major proceeded to impress the sugar[45] owned by Savannah too, with the notice that "it matters not to whom the sugar belongs; it is necessary for the subsistence of the armies of the Confederate States in the field, and it is my duty to obtain it."[46] Savannah had paid Yulee between $1.00 and $1.10 per pound for the sugar. To remedy the discrepancy between the price set by the Commissioners in the District of East Florida and the market price actually paid by Savannah, Major Canova suggested, "If, therefore, you wish to submit the law, or your rights under the law, to the consideration of the Court, I, on the part of the government will agree to make up a case and submit the issues between us to his Honor Judge Dawkins, and have our rights determined without delay."[47]

The City of Savannah filed a complaint against Major Canova for the impressments and Yulee for not delivering the sugar. Yulee responded that he was willing to deliver the sugar to Savannah, but was prevented from doing so by Major Canova and the troops stationed at the warehouse. The contract between Yulee and Edgar M. McDonell, Savannah's agent in the transaction, was rescinded, due to Yulee's inability to deliver the sugar.

Judge Dawkins more than doubled the price per pound the CSA commissary had to pay Yulee, from forty-five cents to $1.08. He ruled, "It is therefore ordered, adjudged and decreed that the complaintant, D. L. Yulee, recover of and from the defendant, A. A. Canova, Commissary, &c., the sum of fifty-four thousand two hundred and four dollars and nineteen cents, and interests thereon from the 25th July, A. D. 1863."[48] Yulee appealed this ruling because the market value of sugar had climbed to almost $5.00 per pound and Judge Dawkins had erred by, first, basing his decree on the dollar values arrived at by procedures established under the 1863 Impressment Act and, second, basing the price per pound at the time of actual impressments instead of the day of trial.

Florida Supreme Court Justice Forward reversed Judge Dawkins' ruling and remanded the case back to the trial court with instructions to determine the value of the impressed sugar not according to the procedures established by the Impressment Act, but according to the original agreement between Major Canova and Yulee and for the circuit court, acting as a court of equity, to arrive at a fair market value.

Judge Forward's reasoning had one basic purpose, the protection of property rights. In his opinion Judge Forward adumbrated the legal parameters of the Impressment Act in force when Yulee's sugar was impressed. He concluded that Major Canova was not authorized to circumvent those parameters by contracting with Yulee to submit price disputes to the circuit court:

We ask, wherein then, is this contract connected with a subject fairly within the scope of his [Major Canova's] authority? It is certainly not found in this record. Again, it is not signed by the appellee *officially.* It is true he recognizes it, but it was the act of his attorneys; he recognizes it as a private contract and stipulation. We are forced to the conclusion that the appellee in entering into said contract did not act within the scope of his authority; having done so, it is presumed he acted in his private capacity, and therefore became personally responsible.[49]

Judge Forward acknowledged the "pressing necessities" of the CSA government and commended Major Canova for acting "judiciously under the circumstances." Moreover, Canova's actions recommended a *"moral* claim" for indemnity from the government, since the government sustained no damages as a result of his illegal actions. Nevertheless, the court held Major Canova personally responsible for the unauthorized impressments of Yulee's property. It was the agreement to submit price disputes to the circuit court, acting as a court of equity, that made Major Canova's official titles merely *descripto personae* (more than one legal character, such as army officer and private businessman). In other words, he could not officially act as both a private businessman and a major in the CSA Army. As a private business matter, the dispute could have been resolved by a state court of equity, but CSA impressment disputes were not authorized by CSA law to be resolved in such a manner.

Citing Joseph Story's "Commentaries on Equity Jurisprudence" and US Supreme Court case law, Judge Forward concluded that Judge Dawkins' trial court had jurisdiction because the private parties, Yulee and Canova, agreed to submit to the state equity court. And although the impressment was a federal question, the state court had jurisdiction because, based "upon the principles of natural justice, Courts of Equity might proceed much farther, and might insist upon decreeing a specific performance of all *bona fide* contracts, since that is a remedy to which courts of law are inadequate."[50]

For Judge Forward the final question to be resolved was the legal standard to determine just compensation[51] for Yulee. The CSA insisted that it should be the value on the date of the impressments, July 1863, whereas the property owner insisted upon using the day of the trial in the state court, May 1864. Judge Forward instructed the lower court that "in all contracts for the sale of goods, the price to be fixed therefore, where no price is agreed upon, is the value thereof, quality and quantity considered, on the day of the sale and delivery."[52]

These cases are clear examples of state judicial interposition against unconstitutional CSA attempts to procure what it considered to be necessary supplies for CSA armies in the field. What is most notable is that all of the parties deferred to the rule of law promulgated by the state courts.

❧ III ☙

Habeas corpus is an ancient right of English common law utilized to determine if a prisoner is being unlawfully denied his liberty. "The most common form of this writ is *habeas corpus ad subjiciendum,* directed to the person detaining another, and commanding him to produce the body of the prisoner, or person detained."[53] As is the case with its US counterpart, the CSA Constitution stipulates, "The privilege of the writ of habeas corpus shall not be suspended, unless when in cases of rebellion or invasion the public safety may require it."[54] As the war progressed so too did pressures to suspend the writ of habeas corpus. Those pressures stemmed from a variety of sources, including suspected treason, dealing with the chaos that military forces brought to an area, and the incapacity of the courts, due to the absence of judicial personnel, to process cases. Habeas corpus became especially problematical in the CSA with regard to conscription.

The Provisional Congress early in the conflict questioned the Davis administration about the authority under which citizens were being held by the military. For example, on January 13, 1862, the Congress passed the following resolution: "Resolved, That the President be requested to communicate to Congress by what authority and under what law citizens of Tennessee are imprisoned at Tuscaloosa or other points in the State of Alabama, and whether said prisoners or any portion of them have been transported beyond the limits of their own State without a trial, and whether in any instance the writ of habeas corpus has been suspended."[55] On February 27, 1862, the CSA House and Senate authorized President Davis to suspend "the writ of habeas corpus in certain cases [when required by the public safety]," such authorization to expire thirty days after the next session of Congress. If the Congress failed to reauthorize the suspension within thirty days into the new session, it would expire.[56]

Although the suspension of the writ of habeas corpus is distinct from the establishment of martial law, through which military commanders administer and oversee all civil matters, President Davis did acknowledge a de facto martial law. Even in the absence of prohibitory legislation against the imposition of martial law, President Davis knew that the Congress was mostly opposed to it. Nevertheless, when habeas corpus was suspended and de facto martial law imposed, the state courts had a remarkable presence in curtailing both. As President Davis communicated to the Congress on October 8, 1862, "It will be observed that in some cases, in addition to the suspension of the writ of habeas corpus, all civil jurisdiction (with the exception specified) was also suspended. But the criminal jurisdiction of the ordinary courts has been in no instance interfered with, their action in all such cases being regarded as an assistance and not an obstacle to the military authorities in accomplishing the purposes of the proclamations."[57]

The Davis administration stood amidst the clashing waves of the practical necessity to centralize power and resources to fight a much more numerous and better-equipped adversary, and a community of States adamantly committed to States' rights. In the absence of the CSA Supreme Court, the state supreme courts functioned as the breakers of the raging storm.

In the Matter of J. C. Bryan, Supreme Court of North Carolina

The April 1862 CSA Conscription Act conscripted all men between the ages of eighteen and thirty-five. J. C. Bryan was discharged from service in July 1862 when he was able to procure a thirty-nine-year-old substitute. Following the second CSA Conscription Act, Bryan was arrested in June 1863 as a CSA conscript and delivered to Camp Holmes, a rendezvous for conscripts near Raleigh, because his substitute was conscripted under the September 1862 Conscription Act. While under detention by the CSA military under the authority of the

CSA government, Bryan petitioned in state court for a writ of habeas corpus seeking his release.

The state court issued the writ demanding the release of Bryan. The CSA government appealed to the North Carolina Supreme Court on the grounds that state courts lack jurisdiction to issue such writs against the CSA government. The North Carolina Supreme Court disagreed and upheld the decision of the lower state court that "a person liable to military service, as a conscript, under the Act of Congress of April, 1862, and who, by virtue of the 9th section of the act, regularly procured a discharge by furnishing a proper substitute cannot again be enrolled as a conscript under the act of September, 1862."[58]

Counsel for Bryan viewed the state courts as the "great palladium of personal liberty" against the "seductions or menaces of power," that is, the power of the central government, even in the most extreme emergencies.[59] Whereas counsel for the CSA reiterated the nationalistic reasoning of Chief Justice Marshall, arguing, "The true question is, has a state court the right, by Writ of Habeas Corpus, or otherwise, to interfere with and thwart officers of the Confederate States, acting in the exercise of authority under a law of that government? The right is denied as incompatible with the general powers granted by the constitution to that government, which government would become inefficient in its action, and soon fall into contempt, were the right generally exercised."[60]

Both sides relied on theoretical and case-law precedents to support their positions. Nevertheless, the decisions and actions by the North Carolina courts were essentially reversals of the national judicial supremacy rulings that placed national case-law uniformity and administrative efficiency as higher priorities than the States' obligations to protect the fundamental rights of their respective citizens. In the North Carolina Supreme Court's opinion, the judge wrote:

> We have devoted to the subject that temperate and mature deliberation which its great importance called for, and the Court is of the opinion that it has jurisdiction and is bound to exercise it, and to discharge the citizen whenever it appears that he is unlawfully restrained of his liberty by an officer of the Confederate States. If the restraint is lawful, the court dismisses the application and remands the party. If, on the other hand, the restraint is unlawful, the court discharges him. The lawfulness

or unlawfulness of the restraint necessarily involves the construction of the act of Congress under which the officer justifies the arrest, and the naked question is, by whom is the act of Congress to be construed? By the Secretary of War and the subordinate officers he appoints in order to carry the conscription acts into effect, or by the Judiciary? Or if the latter, have the State courts jurisdiction over the subject? This is a dry question of Constitutional Law. . . . I set forth the power of State Judges to put a construction upon acts of Congress, so far as they involve the rights of the citizen.[61]

The court reaffirmed that it was constrained by the "supremacy clause" of Article VI, that "acts of Congress made in pursuance of the constitution, are the supreme law of the land," and that "it follows that such an act would be as imperative on the State courts and Judges, as on the tribunals of the Confederate States."[62] It strictly interpreted those constraints as instructions to state judges to give full effect to acts made in pursuance of the national constitution, even when in conflict with state laws. But the supremacy clause was not construed to deny state courts concurrent jurisdiction with CSA courts; moreover, the CSA Constitution's supremacy clause placed state supreme courts at parity with the CSA Supreme Court in exercising judicial review. This parity partly explains why the CSA Supreme Court, though authorized to be created, was never formally organized by the CSA Congress. An organized CSA Supreme Court would be redundant, not to mention problematical if conflict between it and state supreme courts arose.

The North Carolina Supreme Court viewed state concurrent jurisdiction with the CSA courts as "a *sacred trust* [emphasis added] [that] has no discretion and no right to be influenced by considerations growing out of the condition of our country, but must act with a single eye to the due administration of the law . . . protecting all her citizens in the full and free enjoyment of life, liberty, and private property."[63]

State, ex rel. Dawson, in re Strawbridge & Mays

An August 1863 CSA law exempted from military service overseers and agriculturalists on farms and plantations, if conscription resulted in no white male adult and left twenty or more able-bodied slaves between the ages of sixteen and fifty on the farm or plantation. A February 1864 CSA law lowered the number of able-bodied slaves to fifteen.[64]

Strawbridge and Mays were conscripted enrollees in the CSA army in Alabama, exempted due to the 1864 law, as they met the statutory requirements for two different farms/plantations. Their employers had to provide bonds verifying that the applied-for exemptions complied with the statutory requirements and that, within twelve months, the farms or plantations would provide for CSA impressments of 100 pounds of bacon and 100 pounds of beef for each able-bodied slave, whether or not said slaves work in the fields. The primary purpose of exempting otherwise eligible conscripts such as Strawbridge and Mays was to keep agricultural productivity at high enough levels for the CSA commissary to procure food supplies.

Nevertheless, the States and the CSA desperately needed to fill their military ranks. The legal question addressed by the Alabama Supreme Court was the state's right to conscript into the state militia persons exempted from military service of the CSA. Obviously, being exempted from the CSA military but yet conscripted into the state militia would impair the capacity of Strawbridge and Mays to fulfill the impressment conditions set forth in the CSA statute. The lower Alabama trial court discharged Strawbridge and Mays from the custody of Captain Dawson of the Alabama militia and the state appealed the discharge.

Writing for the Alabama Supreme Court, Justice Phelan opined that "the question is one of construction," because Alabama law, enacted August 29, 1863, only conferred exemption from state militia service to those exempted under the August 1863 CSA law, not the 1864 law. Acknowledging the difficulty of the issue, he stated that the "precise question is—does the State law just quoted, exempting overseers, relate to and embrace only acts of the Confederate congress then in existence; or, does it also relate to and include acts of the Confederate States which might be subsequently enacted, exempting overseers?"[65] For if the court were to permit the subsequent 1864 CSA law to control, that would essentially allow the CSA Congress to modify the 1863 Alabama law that set twenty able-bodied slaves, not fifteen, as the benchmark for exemption, thereby allowing the CSA to supersede the legislative intent of the Alabama legislature. On the other hand, not to allow the CSA 1864 law to control would be permitting Alabama to thwart CSA legislative intent.

Justice Phelan turned to the Massachusetts Supreme Court for two jurisprudential maxims and a "reasonable construction." Phelan set down those maxims and his analysis as follows:

1. That the natural import of the words of any legislative act, according to the common use of them, when applied to the subject-matter of them, is to be considered as expressing the intention of the legislature, unless the intention so resulting from the ordinary import of the words be repugnant to sound, acknowledged principles of public policy.
2. And if that intention be repugnant to such principles of national policy, then, the import of the words ought to be enlarged, or restrained, so that it may comport with those principles, unless the intention of the legislature be clearly repugnant to them. For, although it is not to be presumed, that a legislature will violate principles of public policy, yet, an intention of the legislature repugnant to those principles, clearly, manifestly, and constitutionally expressed, must have the force of law. A court which will fairly carry out these maxims I do not think can greatly err in construing a statute.[66]

These two Massachusetts judicial maxims sanction the supremacy of state legislative interposition of national policy, when the state legislative intent is "repugnant to those [national] principles, clearly, manifestly, and constitutionally expressed." When those conditions are met, state legislative intent "must have the force of law," national laws notwithstanding. Moreover, it is the duty of the state courts to give sanction to those state laws.[67]

After a lengthy analysis of the Alabama legislature's intent when passing the August 1863 law, the Alabama Supreme Court concluded that it was not the intention of the state legislature to permit its subsequent amendment by the 1864 CSA law. The court reversed the lower court decision by dismissing the writ of habeas corpus and declared Strawbridge and Mays to be liable to the lawful control of Captain Dawson.[68]

Chief Justice Walker noted that this decision was consistent with the principle of national supremacy, as articulated in *McCulloch v. Maryland* (1819). He maintained that in *McCulloch v. Maryland*, national supremacy relates only to "agencies or instruments created by the government of the United States, and not to persons or property within the jurisdiction of a State, and protected by its laws and government." In his opinion, national supremacy was not intended to incapacitate the States to "exert their attributes of sovereignty in reference to any other instruments, than the institutions or agencies created by the general government for the execution of its powers."[69]

Conceding that the central government has the benefit of national supremacy, C. J. Walker expanded the "judgment and discretion" of the state legislature on questions of public policy important to the state.[70] Acknowledging his dismay that denying the writ of habeas corpus to Strawbridge and Mays would impair the CSA's efforts to procure supplies for its armies, he nevertheless concluded that he was constitutionally required to defer to the intent of the state legislature.[71]

Justice Stone dissented from his two colleagues by pragmatically addressing the balance of power between the central and state governments. He reasoned, "State law, though constitutional, if it cannot have operation without coming into collision with the act of congress thus constitutionally enacted, must, for the time, yield the precedence to this supreme law. Such the constitution expressly declares, and we must all obey."[72] Because the CSA needs to exempt able-bodied men from military service in order to provide supplies to the army, the state cannot constitutionally obstruct those pursuits by enrolling them into the state militia. He expansively interprets the relevant CSA statutes in such a way that even though the CSA Congress used the term "exemption," it is in effect a military detail procuring supplies for the army. Due to the supremacy clause and congressional intent behind the term exemption, i.e., military detail, Strawbridge and Mays were not subject to state militia service and were properly discharged by the lower court's writ of habeas corpus.[73]

The two justices in the majority utilized rules of construction that constrained the court's capacity for activist judicial review. Even though the decision resulted in a collision between national and state policy objectives, they did not venture to mitigate that collision by giving the words of the relevant statutes new meanings; nor did they broaden the scope of the central government's delegated powers for practical purposes. The dissenting justice, however, was much more pragmatic in his jurisprudence and used judicial review to essentially mitigate the negative effects of sloppy statutory wording and the wartime inconveniences of a Confederate distribution of delegated and reserved powers.

Burroughs v. Peyton and Abrahams v. Peyton

These jointly decided 1864 Virginia cases involve the power of the CSA Congress to raise and support armies and the power of the CSA to conscript state officials into the CSA military. The cases not only address the rights of individuals, but States' rights vis-à-vis national security. The court focused on the constitutionality of the two 1862 CSA conscription acts, and was prepared to "declare them void and of no effect, however disastrous may be the consequences of [the] decision."[74]

Prioritizing the legal issues raised by the case, Judge Robertson addressed the power of the CSA government to conscript a citizen of a state into the ranks of the CSA Army. Such a power subjects the "personal freedom of every citizen to arbitrary discretion; and moreover [is] inconsistent with the rights of the states; putting their very existence at the mercy of the Confederate government." He maintained that such a power in the hands of any government is dangerous, but nevertheless at times essential to the preservation of liberty. The real question is not if the conscription power exists, but whether it exists at the national or state level. Has the power been delegated to the CSA government by the States, or was the power reserved by the States?[75]

Judge Robertson maintained that the implied legislative conscription power exists in the US Constitution. Prior to the adoption of the US Constitution, the States had the power of conscription during the Revolutionary War, as a "means used for filling the ranks of the regular continental army." This state power was considered to be misplaced, so the framers of the US Constitution placed it with the national government, with the "full power to make war in the Federal government."

Pres. James Madison, through his secretary of state James Monroe, proposed to the Congress a conscription act during the War of 1812. The proposal was dropped when "the treaty of peace with Great Britain rendered the passage of [a conscription act] unnecessary." According to Judge Robertson, the power of the US Congress to pass a conscription act was agreed to exist under the US Constitution, "especially by the southern States of the late union." In the absence of language denying this power to the CSA Congress, the court felt compelled to rule that the CSA government's power of conscription was constitutional.[76]

Both J. R. F. Burroughs and L. P. Abrahams claimed that even if the conscription power was declared to be constitutional, the CSA Congress impaired the obligation of contract when the 1862 April act was superseded by the amendatory 1862 September Act, by subjecting both men to the draft even though they supplied substitutes for the first April act. Moreover, both men claimed to be entitled to just compensation for the costs of their substitutes.

First, the court reasoned that neither man was entitled to just compensation, because the CSA complied with the terms of the April act by receiving their respective substitutes. The September act was in response to changing national circumstances. Exercising judicial restraint, the court maintained:

> The [September] act putting an end to the exemption from military service of those who have furnished substitutes, commences with the recital "Whereas in the present circumstances of the country it requires the aid of all who are able to bear arms;" thus showing, on its face, that but for the pressing necessity of the country the exemption would not have been taken away. It would be beyond the jurisdiction of this court to enquire whether Congress was right or wrong in supposing such necessity to exist. Of its existence, Congress, to whose discretion it is confided to provide means adequate to the defence of the country, has the exclusive right to judge."[77]

Second, the constitutional prohibition against "impairing the obligation of contracts" applies only to state governments, as noted in Article I, section 10. The framers of both the US and CSA constitutions intentionally omitted that clause from application to their national governments in Article I, section 9. Nevertheless, "the truth seems to be that substitution was permitted as an act of grace and favor on the part of the government, and not as a matter of contract." And even Burroughs, who procured his substitute under a February 1862 state law, was not thereby exempted from the draft if the circumstances should require "the aid of all who are able to bear arms." Citing US Supreme Court precedent, the court concluded, "The well established rule of construction is that all grants of privileges and exemptions from general burdens are to be construed liberally and in favor of the public and strictly as against the grantee. Whatever is not plainly expressed and unequivocally granted is to be taken to have been withheld." And because the April Conscription Act did not "plainly express and unequivocally grant" that substitutes would exempt Burroughs and Abrahams for the duration of the war, and the public necessity required their service, the September act did not breach a contract.[78]

Third, the court mentions a practical reason as well. Conscription was a bulwark against a centralized government determined to assail States' rights, whereas voluntary and mercenary armies pose serious threats. The court reasoned:

There was no serious reason to apprehend that a government designing to overthrow the liberties of the people, would raise an army for the purpose, by a conscription of the very people whose rights were to be assailed; and it was obvious that if it should have the folly to do so, the army, when raised, would be the most efficient instrument that could be devised, for the defeat of the object in view. The danger really apprehended, from the grant of the power to raise and support armies, was that the Federal government would be enabled to raise and keep in its pay an army of mercenary troops with no interests in common with the people; which might be used for the overthrow of their liberties and the destruction of the rights of the states. . . . The power to raise armies by conscription is less dangerous to the liberties of the people, than is the power of raising them by voluntary enlistment. An improper exercise of the power of conscription could not fail to excite at once the indignant opposition of the people; while an army might be improperly increased by voluntary enlistment without attracting much popular attention; and one thus raised would, as has been shown, be much more dangerous to the rights of the States, and the liberties of the people, than the one raised by conscription.[79]

And, fourth, the States have the prerogative to interpose and nullify CSA conscription laws. The best constitutional security against the CSA government abusing its conscription powers is the States themselves, and their respective republican forms of government. The Confederate government's conscription powers do not extend to state executive, legislative, and judicial officers. "[The CSA] Congress can have no such power over state officers. The state governments are an essential part of [the] political system; upon the separate and independent sovereignty of the states the foundation of [the] Confederacy rests."[80] Moreover, it is the "reserved right of each state to resume the powers delegated to the Confederate government, whenever, in her judgment, they are perverted to the injury or oppression of her people."[81]

John Barnes v. John T. Barnes

This case relates to property rights and addresses the constitutionality of North Carolina's "Stay Law," which suspended civil trials requiring juries, warrants before a justice of the peace in suits or actions for debt, demands on bonds, promissory notes, bills of exchange, covenants for the payment of money, judgments, accounts, and all contracts for money demands or for specific articles.[82] In other words, it protected debtors from creditors during the war.

Chief Justice Pearson maintained that the court lacked the right to decide whether or not the Stay Law was an expedient and appropriate legislative response to a state emergency. Rather, the court's responsibility is to give judgment on the constitutionality of the legislature passing the law. The court concluded that both the US and CSA constitutions prohibited the state from passing any such law that impairs the obligation of contracts. And even though North Carolina was not a member of the CSA when the Stay Law was passed, and the CSA Constitution's proscription uses the future tense "no State *shall* [emphasis added] pass any law," such is "a play upon words, and is not worthy of the gravity of the subject."[83]

Apart from the CSA Constitution, North Carolina's Stay Law violates the state constitution on two grounds. First, the North Carolina declaration of rights stipulates that "no free man ought to be deprived of his life, liberty, or property, but by the law of the land." The Stay Law was a legislative deprivation of creditors' vested property rights. "Manifestly, if a creditor is deprived of his right to have judgment and execution for his debt, he is thereby deprived of his right to his debt, which consists in his right to enforce payment. . . . Because the power to deprive one of his debt for an indefinite time is the same as the power to deprive him of it absolutely."[84]

And second, the Stay Law is unconstitutional because it violates the separation of powers between the North Carolina legislative and judicial branches. Chief Justice Pearson postulated that the assertion and exercise of such a legislative power would "destroy the independence of the executive and supreme judicial powers of the government, and subvert the government established by the constitution, by centering all powers of the Legislative department, and making a despotism, instead of a free government where the powers are divided and given to separate departments, each acting in its appropriate sphere, as a check on the other." He continued:

> A power to suspend or abolish the administration of justice, cannot exist in a free government. . . . [The] state constitution gives ample protection to its citizens against all encroachments on the part of the Legislature upon the rights of property. . . . For in truth, no government can be free, unless the Constitution provides for the protection of property, the due administration of the law and the independence of the supreme judicial department.[85]

Juaraqui v. The State

In this criminal case, which relates to due process, the conviction of Juaraqui was overturned by the Texas Supreme Court on a technicality. The defendant had been indicted for perjury and convicted.

In his ruling for the defendant, Judge Wheeler determined that the indictment did not include the statutory definition of perjury. The statutory definition states, "Perjury is a false statement, either written or verbal, deliberately and willfully made, relating to something past or present, under the sanction of an oath, or such affirmation as is by law equivalent to an oath, where such an oath or affirmation is legally administered, under circumstances in which an oath or affirmation is required by law, or is necessary for the prosecution or defense of any private right, or for the ends of public justice."

The indictment averred that the defendant did "falsely, wickedly, willfully and corruptly, in manner and form aforesaid, commit willful and corrupt perjury." The court ruled the indictment to be defective because it deviated from the statutory definition of perjury. By not using the statutory definition of perjury, the grand jury had to deduce that the defendant committed perjury according to the Texas penal code. As a result, the court reversed Juaraqui's conviction and remanded the case back to the trial court with the stipulation the trial proceed with the statutory definition of perjury.[86]

⋈ IV ⋈

One can only speculate as to the long-term impact of slaves being accorded due process rights in state courts within the CSA, had the CSA survived the war. Based upon the historic role the courts have played in securing fundamental rights, it is reasonable to suggest that they would have continued the expansion of fundamental rights. Court rulings involving the plight of slaves have acted as potent solvents to the peculiar institution in both Northern and Southern States. In the absence of Northern agitation within the old Union,[87] international and domestic political and economic pressures would have fueled gradual manumission in the CSA. Abolitionism probably would have once again emerged as a viable political force within the CSA, and state courts would have been important forums for litigating against slave owners where slavery and the rule of law intersected.

Gradual manumission even took hold within the CSA Congress, when in 1865 it approved a bill that stipulated "all slaves received into the service under the provisions of this act shall be valued and paid for according to existing laws, and that said slaves, or any of them, shall be manumitted by general orders from the War Department, if the consent of the State in which the said slaves may be at the time is given for their manumission."[88]

It is highly noteworthy that the Fourteenth Amendment due process rights of life, liberty, and property for freed blacks had precedence in Southern States as manifested in cases involving slaves. In other words, slaves had due process rights within the CSA, which would certainly have been expanded first in the Border States and then throughout the Confederacy. The following sample of cases makes this quite clear.

Josephine [a Slave] v. Mississippi

This Mississippi Supreme Court case addressed the legality of the indictment and subsequent conviction of a slave named Josephine for the capital murder of fourteen-month-old Lelia Virginia Jones by arsenic poisoning. Lafayette Jones, the father and Josephine's owner, was in a sexual relationship with Josephine. In an act of revenge directed towards the Jones family, Josephine poisoned Mrs. Jones and Lelia with arsenic-laced tea.

The first trial in 1857 ended when the judge dismissed the jury, due to its inability to render a verdict in the waning minutes of the last day the trial court could legally sit. In the attempt to have the murder charges against her dropped, Josephine's lawyer unsuccessfully argued that, under Mississippi law, judges lack the power in capital cases, without sufficient legal necessity, to discharge the jury on the grounds that it is unable to reach a verdict. "Such discharge upon that ground alone would entitle the defendant to a discharge, and would operate as an acquittal."[89] A second trial was held in 1858, in which Josephine was convicted. Her counsel appealed the conviction to the state supreme court in 1861.

The issues were multiple and complex, but the appeal can be broken down into the following: Is the indictment void, first because "no time is alleged in said indictment with certainty when said Lelia Virginia Jones drank and swallowed the mentioned tea in the indictment"; second, because it is not averred in the indictment that the "said Lelia or any other human being died of the poison charged to have been administered"; third, because the trial court lacked jurisdiction; fourth, because of the disqualification of a juror; fifth, because of the refusal of continuances; sixth, because of the exclusion of evidence by the trial court judge that Mr. Jones had engaged in sexual relations with his slaves Eliza and Josephine, the exclusion of which was prejudicial to the defendant; seventh, because the second trial was a violation of the state constitutional protection against double jeopardy; eighth, because discharging the jury in the first trial without legal necessity was an acquittal for the defendant; and ninth, because the judge's instruction to the jury "that under the laws of this State, and the laws which are to govern them in their investigation of this case, make all accessories, before the fact, to the commission of murder, principals, and punishes them with the same penalties imposed on principals" was illegal under Mississippi law?[90]

The Mississippi Supreme Court ordered a third trial for Josephine, thereby overturning her conviction in the second trial. Justice Handy concluded that disallowing the prisoner's counsel to interrogate Mr. Jones about the alleged poisoning of his first wife by his slave Eliza, with whom he was having sexual relations at the time, and the alleged statement by Eliza that she would soon put Mrs. Jones underground, "were clearly irrelevant," because her location on the plantation at the time of the crime provided no opportunity for her to commit the crime. Additionally, not allowing examination of Mr. Jones' habit of sexual intercourse with Eliza and Josephine was not prejudicial to Josephine, but beneficial. Justice Handy reasoned that evidence of sexual relations between Mr. Jones and Josephine "was a sufficient answer to the imputation of malice on her part against Mrs. Jones."[91] Acknowledging a substantial right of the slave Josephine, Justice Handy opined:

> The matter here involved was a substantial right of the prisoner and not a mere question of form of proceeding. By the law in force at the time of the commission of the alleged crime, she was not subject to conviction as an accessory before the fact, upon the indictment charging her only as a principal, but was entitled to be informed by the indictment what degree of guilt she was charged with, and what

offence in law she was called to answer. This was a valuable right. But to make the statute under consideration applicable to her case would be to impair the right of defence existing by the law in force at the time the act was committed; and this we think it clear the Legislature did not intend to do. If this view be correct, it follows that the instructions are erroneous in the particulars stated above.[92]

Justice Handy, not questioning the sufficiency of the evidence to sustain the guilty verdict, overturned the verdict because it is unclear if a juror based his verdict on the belief that Josephine was a principal or accessory. Because the indictment was based upon Josephine being the principal, state law precluded a conviction as an accessory not charged in the indictment. The facts of the trial court and the testimony of the witnesses provide substantial evidence of Josephine's guilt. Nevertheless, the legal community and system within Mississippi provided three trials in which the fundamental rights of the slave Josephine were acknowledged and adjudicated, in spite of the mountain of evidence supporting the murder charges.

Elvira, a Slave, Supreme Court of Virginia

In April 1864 Elvira, a slave and the property of C. Ford, was tried and convicted *en banc* by four of the five trial court justices for attempting to poison the Ford family. One justice dissented from the court's opinion and judgment. The felony conviction left the court with one of two sentences: execution or sale and deportation from the CSA. The court sentenced Elvira to the latter. After the sentencing C. Ford petitioned the Circuit Court of Petersburg for a writ of habeas corpus and to have Elvira discharged from custody. The petition claimed that state law required that convictions carrying a sentence of death had to be by the unanimous opinion of all five justices and that one dissenting justice amounts to an acquittal of the defendant. The circuit court denied his petition.

Ford appealed to the Virginia Supreme Court. Justice Moncure reasoned that the legislature's intent and the language of the relevant state laws stipulate that "unanimity was necessary to the conviction of a slave for [a capital] offense." He wrote, "The meaning of the words in the Code, ch. 212, (5, 'No slave shall be condemned to death nor a free Negro to the penitentiary, unless all the justices sitting on his trial agree in the sentence,' in my view is, that 'no slave shall be convicted in an offense punishable with death unless all the justices shall agree in the judgment of conviction."[93] He concluded, "The offence for which the slave Elvira was tried being punishable by death, and all the parties who sat on her trial not having agreed in her conviction, she was therefore, in effect, acquitted. It follows that I am for reversing the judgment of the Circuit court and rendering a judgment to discharge her from imprisonment and restore her to the possession of her owner."[94]

Jones & Daugharty v. Aaron Goza

In this Louisiana Supreme Court case, the plaintiffs filed suit to recover $600 in legal fees from the slave's owner for assisting in the defense of a slave charged with murder. Due to the efforts of the law firm of Jones & Daugharty, the jury acquitted the slave. In the absence of the slave's owner at the time of the trial, and in accordance with Louisiana law, the slave was entitled to legal counsel at state expense. The magistrate had appointed A. J. Lawrence, Esq., to represent the defendant for a fee of $50 and also assented to having Jones & Daugharty assist in the defense. Judge Land ruled that the magistrate exceeded his legal authority by assigning additional counsel for the accused, thereby binding the accused to additional legal fees: "It is not pretended that there was any express contract for the payment of fees; and the only ground on which the plaintiffs can claim compensation for their services, is that they appeared, and assisted in the case, with the consent of the magistrate before whom the slave was tried. . . . There is no legal ground on which the present action for the recovery of compensation can be maintained. . . . And it is now ordered, adjudged and decreed, that the plaintiffs' demands be rejected, with costs in both courts."[95] Not only was the defendant slave acquitted in a jury trial, but her attorneys successfully represented her on what amounted to *pro bono* legal counsel.

❧ V ❧

If "necessity is the supreme lawmaker," an amazing fact about the Confederate judicial system is the documentary evidence of its strict adherence to the rule of law. There was not a military despotism, nor a de facto termination of fundamental rights. When and where the courts could operate, they administered justice with clarity, consistency, and honor, almost, one could argue, to a fault considering the circumstances. The CSA Constitution was upheld without national judicial supremacy, but within a Confederate model in which and through which States' rights-based self-government was the "necessity" that culminated as the "supreme lawmaker." Had Lincoln's war not interrupted the evolution of the CSA, strong evidence suggests that Confederate justice would have been effectively administered through a decentralized court system adamantly adhering to the rule of law.

Chapter III

EXECUTIVE POWER

I have had occasion more than once to express, and deem it now proper to repeat, that it is, in my judgment, to be taken for granted, as a fundamental proposition not requiring elucidation, that the federal government is the creature of the individual States, and of the people of the States severally; that the sovereign power was in them alone.

Pres. Franklin Pierce, 1855 veto message

***

The Chief Magistrate derives all his authority from the people, and they have referred none upon him to fix terms for the separation of the States. The people themselves can do this if also they choose, but the Executive as such has nothing to do with it. His duty is to administer the present Government as it came to his hands and to transmit it unimpaired by him to his successor.

Pres. Abraham Lincoln, 1861 Inaugural Address

❧ I ❧

In November of 1852, *The American Whig Review* remarked, "There perhaps was never a political assemblage the results of which were more entirely committed to chance, than the late Democratic National Convention. . . . All at once, in the twinkling of an eye, Franklin Pierce turned up with the Presidential card in his hands, and then the exclamation instantly burst from thousands of lips, *Who is Franklin Pierce?*"[1]

That question is still being asked today. A current biographer begins his tome with "Who was Franklin Pierce? Why in the world would anyone write about his presidency?" Pierce's ignominy is explained a few sentences later: "[He] remained loyal to the Democratic party even when it was tarred with the brush of treason during the Civil War—a war he refused to support—and he was himself accused of Confederate sympathies. That was enough to destroy his later reputation."[2] One thing is certain about the presidency of Franklin Pierce; it is inextricably linked to the events of 1860 to 1865.

The unfavorable scholarly assessments of the Pierce administration form the pedestal upon which scholarship has placed President Lincoln. More precisely, Lincoln's reputation as a great president has less to do with adherence to the American rule of law and more to do with his leadership in reversing Southern secession through the rule *by* law. President Pierce's reputation as a presidential dud, on the other hand, is in reality an implicit condemnation of presidential adherence to the traditional American rule *of* law. Both, however, should be evaluated according to the manner and extent to which they complied with the American rule of law. To do otherwise is an implicit endorsement of the arbitrary rule of men, "the very definition of tyranny."[3]

The fact that Lincoln consistently ranks as a great president and Pierce as one of the most inept is substantially attributable to placing presidential greatness outside the confines of the rule of law.[4]

It is clear that the legacy of the "mythic and majestic" Lincoln stems from his willingness to dispense with the rule of law in order to achieve political objectives favorable to the dominant political class, then and now. Wrecking decentralized federalism, opening the doors to ever-increasing centralization, legitimizing the rhetoric of abstract egalitarianism,[5] and transforming the presidency into a Caesarean promoter of empire are important elements of Lincoln's legacy. To claim that upholding the traditional American rule of law is the core of Lincoln's legacy is not only implausible, but laughable. Even his handling of the slavery issue was unconstitutional, opportunistic, disingenuous, and left the emancipated freedmen at the mercy of a decimated South and a racist America.[6]

Because Lincoln's legacy is firmly linked to the victorious Union Army does not necessarily make it a positive good. As he responded with bloody coercion to a nation in the process of "fragmenting," he provided the rhetoric and precedent for a fragmented world that many globalists argue needs to be centralized. In the words of Gov. Mario

Cuomo, "Lincoln speaks today not only to his own countrymen but also to his brothers and sisters worldwide. . . . Shouldn't we be equally interested in measuring our potential decisions against those he might have made?"[7] Mr. Cuomo maintains that Lincoln is the role model for achieving justice in the US: "Whatever is calculated to advance the condition of the honest, struggling, laboring man, so far as my judgment will enable me to judge of a correct thing, I am for that thing." But the application is now global: "But more than that, to the extent that we deem ourselves comfortable here at home, should we not consider devoting a larger portion of our abundance than we have so far to those desperately needy in foreign lands living on the same globe we all occupy as the great family of men?"[8] According to Cuomo, Lincoln's legacy matters because it is instrumental in blazing the trail for global centralization. Providing the United Nations with ever-increasing powers cannot be squared with the democratic-republican ideals of the framers, but only rationalized to promote so-called noble humanitarian purposes of global egalitarianism and redistribution of wealth.

The globalist aspirations of Governor Cuomo notwithstanding, Lincoln's record on upholding the traditional American rule of law is problematical. The politicians who seek guidance from Lincoln must be willing to forego the traditional American rule of law in the quest to maximize the political power needed to achieve their policy objectives. Such guidance is not sought from Pierce, whose record is essentially one of a strict adherence to the American rule of law, States' rights, and decentralization.

Both presidents presided over constitutional crises with opportunities to uphold or diminish the rule of law. Lincoln's story is a familiar one. The tug came, and he pulled back with a vengeance, roping the States into a unified whole. Pierce's obscurity, on the other hand, is due in large measure to his unwillingness to exceed the constitutional limits placed on the executive branch. Preferring Lincoln over Pierce is tantamount to preferring political expediency over the rule of law. Contrasting Pierce's presidential conduct with that of Lincoln's should clarify the distinction between the rule *of* law and the rule *by* law and how much more precarious the former is in Lincoln's America.

❧ II ❧

The decade that preceded the outbreak of military hostilities between Northern and Southern States was in many significant ways a cold-war prelude to the shooting war between North and South. The cold-war posturing between Northern and Southern interests is manifested in the fissures that increasingly separated Northern and Southern approaches to the American rule of law.[9] Sectional disputes over the territories ostensibly were the most serious threat to the union of States, but behind these disputes was competition for control of the central government. The intensity of sectional conflicts over the territories, such as whether Kansas would be admitted into the Union as a free or slave state, was fueled by the larger question of which section would control the national government.

The compromise patched together in 1850 did little to cool the fever of heightened sectionalism that had infected the union of States. To the contrary, it exposed the raw nerves of the body politic, ranging from national fiscal policies to the slavery issue. The 1852 party platforms provide insights into the public policies that were producing an environment unable to support political parties with national appeal. The national political parties were becoming sectionalized, in the pursuit of regional over national interests.

The salient policy issues during the 1852 presidential election are adumbrated in the Democratic Party Platform of 1852, the planks of which candidate and later president Pierce stood upon throughout his presidency:

Plank 1. Expanding National Powers: That the federal government is one of limited powers, derived solely from the constitution, and the grants of power made therein ought to be strictly construed by all the departments and agents of the government; and that it is inexpedient and dangerous to exercise doubtful constitutional powers.

Plank 2. Internal Improvements: That the constitution does not confer upon the general government the power to commence and carry on a general system of internal improvements.

Plank 3. State Debts: That the constitution does not confer authority upon the federal government, directly or indirectly, to assume the debts of the several States, contracted for local and internal improvements or other State purposes; nor would such assumption be just or expedient.

Plank 4. Protectionism: That justice and sound policy forbid the federal government to foster one branch of industry to the detriment of any other, or to cherish the interests of one portion to the injury of another portion of our common country; that every citizen, and every section of the country, has a right to demand and insist upon an equality of rights and privileges, and to complete an ample protection of person and property from domestic violence or foreign aggression.

Plank 5. Fiscal Responsibility: That it is the duty of every branch of the government to enforce and practice the most rigid economy in conducting our public affairs, and that no more revenue ought to be raised than is required to defray the necessary expenses of the government, and for the gradual but certain extinction of the public debt.

Plank 6. National Bank: That Congress has no power to charter a national bank; that we believe such an institution one of deadly hostility to the best interests of the country, dangerous to our republican institutions and the liberties of the people, and calculated to place the business of the country within the control of a concentrated money power, and above the laws and the will of the people; and that the results of democratic legislation in this and all other financial measures upon which issues have been made between the two political parties of the country, have demonstrated, to candid and practical men of all parties, their soundness, safety, and utility in all business pursuits.

Plank 7. Federal Banking Deposits: That the separation of the moneys of the government from banking institutions is indispensable for the safety of the funds of the government and the rights of the people.

Plank 8. Nativism: That the liberal principles embodied by Jefferson in the Declaration of Independence, and sanctioned in the constitution, which make ours the land of liberty and the asylum of the oppressed of every nation, have ever been cardinal principles in the democratic faith; and every attempt to abridge the privilege of becoming citizens and the owners of the soil among us ought to be resisted with the same spirit that swept the alien and sedition laws from our statute-books.

Plank 9. Slavery: That Congress has no power under the constitution to interfere with or control the domestic institutions of the several States, and that such States are the sole and proper judges of everything appertaining to their own affairs not prohibited by the constitution; that all efforts of the abolitionists or others made to induce Congress to interfere with questions of slavery, or to take incipient steps in relation thereto, are calculated to lead to the most alarming and dangerous consequences; and that all such efforts have an inevitable tendency to diminish the happiness of the people and endanger the stability and permanency of the Union, and ought not to be countenanced by any friend of our political institutions.[10]

These issues relate to the American rule of law. The traditional rule of law was more favorable to the Democratic status quo positions, whereas it was increasingly viewed as an obstacle to be overcome by Whigs and later the Republicans. This is particularly the case with the "slavery plank," which would prove to test local, state, and national adherence to the rule of law. By emphasizing fundamental rights of the slaves while pursuing policy objectives of questionable constitutionality, such as internal improvements, protectionism, and non-enforcement of fugitive slave laws, the Republicans resorted to a subjective higher law that trumped the rule of law embodied in the US Constitution and diminished its esteem in the North. In the words of the abolitionist William Lloyd Garrison, the Constitution was a "covenant with death and an agreement with hell."[11]

The Republican Party Platform of 1856 had the following policy admonitions and planks:

Resolved: That while the Constitution of the United States was ordained and established by the people, in order to "form a more perfect union, establish justice, insure domestic tranquility, provide for the common defense, promote the general welfare, and secure the blessings of liberty," and contain ample provision for the protection of the life, liberty, and property of every citizen, the dearest Constitutional rights of the people of Kansas have been fraudulently and violently taken from them.
Their Territory has been invaded by an armed force;
Spurious and pretended legislative, judicial, and executive officers have been set over them, by whose usurped authority, sustained by the

military power of the government, tyrannical and unconstitutional laws have been enacted and enforced. . . .

Resolved, That Kansas should be immediately admitted as a state of this Union, with her present Free Constitution, as at once the most effectual way of securing to her citizens the enjoyment of the rights and privileges to which they are entitled, and of ending the civil strife now raging in her territory. . . .

Resolved, That a railroad to the Pacific Ocean by the most central and practicable route is imperatively demanded by the interests of the whole country, and that the Federal Government ought to render immediate and efficient aid in its construction, and as an auxiliary thereto, to the immediate construction of an emigrant road on the line of the railroad.

Resolved, That appropriations by Congress for the improvement of rivers and harbors, of a national character, required for the accommodation and security of our existing commerce, are authorized by the Constitution, and justified by the obligation of the Government to protect the lives and property of its citizens.

Resolved, That we invite the affiliation and cooperation of the men of all parties, however differing from us in other respects, in support of the principles herein declared; and believing that the spirit of our institutions as well as the Constitution of our country, guarantees liberty of conscience and equality of rights among citizens, we oppose all legislation impairing their security.[12]

As the 1852 Democratic and the 1856 Republican party platforms make evident, the Union was dividing along party lines either supporting or opposing national powers on internal improvements, protectionism, and the slavery issues. The capacity of the national institutions to mediate these sectional conflicts was being tested to its limits. Presidential leadership at this juncture would determine the outcome.

Pierce began his presidency with an overly optimistic view of the state of the union. In his 1853 inaugural address he stated, "The controversies which have agitated the country heretofore are passing away with the causes which produced them and the passions which they had awakened."[13]

Pierce was determined to have the "controversies which have agitated the country" resolved at the state level. He did not advance the idea of a proactive role for the national government. If anything, reflecting the Democratic party platform, he advocated rolling back the policy jurisdiction of the national government in order to prevent party lines from becoming irreversibly sectionalized between North and South. He was, in short, a States' rights president. National tensions could be diffused by curtailing the reach of national power, and deferring to the public-policy prerogatives of the States.

This is not meant to imply that he failed to recognize the policy responsibilities of the national government. Where the national government was constitutionally required to act, e.g., the capture of fugitive slaves, the Pierce administration was proactive; in those policy areas lacking constitutional sanction, e.g., internal improvements, the executive branch exercised restraint.

Pierce was not opposed to internal improvements in principle, but such improvements were primarily the policy responsibility of the States. For example, the Democratic Party Platform of 1852 resolved, "That the democratic party will faithfully abide by and uphold the principles laid down in the Kentucky and Virginia resolutions of 1798, and in the report of Mr. Madison to the Virginia legislature in 1799; that it adopts those principles as constituting one of the main foundations of its political creed, and is resolved to carry them out in their obvious meaning and import." Echoing those sentiments, President Pierce announced, "The thirteen States have grown to be thirty-one, with relations reaching to Europe on the one side and on the other to the distant realms of Asia. I am deeply sensible of the immense responsibility which the present magnitude of the Republic and the diversity and multiplicity of its interests devolves upon me, the alleviation of which so far as relates to the immediate conduct of the public business, is, first, in my reliance on the wisdom and patriotism of the two Houses of Congress, and, secondly, in the directions afforded me by the principles of public polity affirmed by our fathers of the epoch of 1798, sanctioned by long experience, and consecrated anew by the overwhelming voice of the people of the United States."[14]

Pierce concluded that he had a mandate from the American electorate to advance the collective interest of the American commercial empire on the one hand, while preserving a consensual union of bickering States on the other. His objective was to contain the bickering within manageable limits, so that it did not escalate to disorder and/or disunion.

Swirling around his presidency were issues to which there were no easy policy solutions. Whether it be the Kansas-Nebraska controversy, slavery, the fugitive slave laws, US expansion into Central America and the Caribbean, the realignment of political parties, or the high-stakes rivalries over a government-subsidized railroad to the Pacific, the competing sectional demands placed Pierce in an extremely unstable political setting. Because Pierce was committed to the American rule of law first and foremost, the shortcomings of his administration in dealing with high-conflict issues should be viewed in light of that commitment. In other words, criticisms of Pierce are essentially misdirected dissatisfaction with the constraints that the American rule of law places on the policy prerogatives of the executive branch of government, such as internal improvements and the fugitive slave laws. The lapse of effective leadership was not at the executive level, but within the US House and Senate.

The fact that Pierce did not exercise unconstitutional powers in an attempt to quell the regional demands on the national government stems from his commitment to the rule of law. This commitment is not a failure of leadership, but rather a type of leadership that placed a higher value on constitutional constraints, i.e., the rule of law, than it did on political expediency.

❈ III ❧

Much of the scholarship critical of Pierce either explicitly or implicitly points to the fact that his administration was rounding up runaway slaves, thereby inflaming sectional hostilities. One critical biographer notes, "Property rights and upholding the law were paramount for him. Seldom was a President so out of touch with popular opinion."[15] But his fiscal conservatism was equally, if not more so, inflammatory to his political opposition.

Opposition to the enforcement of the fugitive slave law was intense in some Northern States. Some of them enacted personal liberty laws and had the assistance of state courts issuing writs of habeas corpus to thwart the efforts of U.S. marshals. The Northern States were engaged in a sub rosa form of state interposition and nullification of national fugitive slave laws.[16] The Pierce administration had to determine the constitutional options of a US president when confronted with state interposition and/or nullification of national laws.

Pierce's constitutional duty to enforce the fugitive slave laws did not diminish his disdain for the institution of slavery. For example, when supporting the congressional passage of the Kansas-Nebraska Bill, he did so not at the behest of Southern States, but in response to the demands of Westerners. Pierce "assured the country that the bill was in the interests of freedom; that not another slave state would ever come into the Union."[17]

In Pierce's mind, popular sovereignty was in effect practical abolition. Pierce's political detractors harangued him for being a proslavery president and a pawn of a Southern slaveocracy. This was a partisan trick to destroy the Democratic party in the North. Political rivals portrayed Pierce's evenhanded dealings with the South as a betrayal of Northern interests. Much of the leadership in the Northern States, particularly New England, had replaced affinity with vitriol for the South by the early 1850s and was determined to remake the South into the image of New England or destroy it. As one historian has noted:

> Throughout the antebellum period, northerners increasingly came to regard the South as a land, and southerners as a people, apart. Rather than constructing a unifying myth of common origins and descent, nineteenth-century Americans were more interested in inventing a myth of *uncommon* descent, a process summed up by the stereotypical images of the southern Cavalier and the northern Yankee. Although it was a fictitious construction—and a destructive one—the idea that the North and South had separate origins helped northerners distance themselves from a society that they saw as an affront to American values. It absolved them, too, of any residual share of the guilt in the maintenance of the South's peculiar institution and conveniently ignored the overt racism of northern society.[18]

In the opinion of the New England elite, the reprobate South had to be Americanized along the New England model. This

"Americanization" of the South would remedy the agrarian backwardness that was proving so problematical for Northern economic interests. That is why the Republican party's "focus was not on the moral wrong of slavery but on the economic, social, and political danger arising from the power of the white, slaveholding inhabitants of the southern states—a power that was expressed by, and drew its strength from, the ownership of slaves."[19] By destroying slavery, the Republicans could undermine the economic power, and consequently the political influence, of the Southern political class.

While the States were increasingly becoming sectionalized and driving the Union asunder, Pierce was desperately trying to keep it intact. His success was contingent upon the viability of the Democratic party as a national party, the effective enforcement of national laws, and the implementation of policies aimed at the collective national interests. Obviously if the enforcement of national laws and policies, such as the fugitive slave laws and conservative fiscal policies, ran counter to regional interests, then the viability of the Democratic party in those regions would be undermined. As Republican party political operatives sought control of the US government, they stoked the flames of regional biases.

Undermining the Democratic party was not a benign process. It was closely related to the success of factions whose policy objectives were being obstructed by the Pierce Democrats. Accordingly, President Pierce's constitutional obligation to "faithfully execute the [fugitive slave] laws of the United States" was resisted not only by those who morally opposed slavery, but also by those opposed to the administration's fiscal policy. In short, the Northern States' opposition to the Pierce administration's enforcement of the fugitive slave laws masked a much broader policy agenda.

That agenda is manifested in Ohio Congressman Campbell's remarks, stemming from his dissatisfaction with the Pierce administration's refusal to approve internal improvements for Western (i.e., Midwestern) States: "No legislation on River and Harbor Appropriations, so much needed by the North—no legislation on the Pacific Railroad, so vital to the interests of our great Commercial States and Atlantic Cities—no Niagara Ship Canal, but Nebraska— enforcing the Fugitive Slave law—filibustering for Cuba and her slaves—increasing the rates of postage is all that the present Administration has at heart."[20] It is highly unlikely that the congressman would have raised a hue and cry about enforcement of the fugitive slave laws in Nebraska had Pierce passed the pork-loaded River and Harbor Bill he so desperately sought.

To the detriment of his political career, Pierce was consistent in his internal improvements policy throughout his presidency, which in turn intensified the determination of his opponents. His internal improvements policy rested upon an unwavering commitment to the constitutionally limited government, constrained by the rule of law. Pierce's opposition to internal improvements, that is, those internal improvements not required by the "exigencies of the naval or military services of the country,"[21] was the constitutional rule of law that deferred to the States' police powers and the efficiencies of free enterprise. Pierce was determined to leash the spending frenzy his predecessors set loose.

Pierce's veto message to the Senate and House regarding the 1854 River and Harbor Bill manifests a thoughtful commitment to principle over political expediency. Pierce was cognizant of the fury that an agitated region could generate when its pet projects were derailed, for whatever reason. He knew that when President Polk vetoed a similar bill it doomed his administration. Now it was Pierce's turn, and his rationale for vetoing the bill did not stem from an ideological anti-internal improvements perspective, but from a constitutional rule of law perspective.

His perspective has two fundamental premises: first, the US government is the agent of the States and, second, the US government is a government of discernible limited powers. Both of these premises were undergoing mutations, as pressure for augmented national government roles in the national economy mounted. In his veto message, Pierce exasperatingly maintained, "I have had occasion more than once to express, and deem it now proper to repeat, that it is, in my judgment, to be taken for granted, as a fundamental proposition not requiring elucidation, that the federal government is the creature of the individual States, and of the people of the States severally; that the sovereign power was in them alone; that all the powers of the federal government are derivative ones, the enumeration and limitations of which are contained in the instrument which organized it, and by express terms. The powers not delegated to the United States by the Constitution, nor prohibited by it to the States, are reserved to the States respectively or to the people."[22]

Operating from the perspective that national government "is the creature of the individual States" and its powers are "derivative" from the States is highly significant, because it places the loci of sovereignties in the respective States, and not in the sovereignty of the American people. The latter model is much more amenable to an expansive interpretation of national powers, such as congressional commerce powers. For example, nationally financed internal improvements obtain constitutional legitimacy through the congressional majorities that passed funding for the various projects. The minority of States opposed to such legislation lack the constitutional grounds to thwart it, being a numerical minority on the losing side of a national public policy debate. Whereas if the national power to authorize and fund internal improvements is individually derivative from the States, that power can be recalled by the States individually through state interposition, nullification, and ultimately state secession. Secession is tantamount to a state's total recall of the powers it delegated to the national government.

Pierce was not opposed to internal improvements per se, but he was opposed to internal improvements with regional biases and not linked to the national government's delegated powers to promote national defense:

> If an appropriation for improving the navigability of a river, or deepening or protecting a harbor, have reference to military or naval purposes, then its rightfulness, whether in the amount or in the objects to which it is applied, depends, manifestly, on the military or naval exigency; and the subject-matter affords its own measure of legislative discretion. But if the appropriation of such an object have no distinct relation to the military or naval wants of the country, and is wholly, or even mainly, intended to promote the revenue from commerce, then the very vagueness of the proposed purpose of the expenditure constitutes a perpetual admonition of reserve and caution. Through disregard of this, it is undeniable that, in many cases, appropriations of this nature have been made unwisely, without accomplishing beneficial results commensurate with

the costs, and sometimes for evil, rather than good, independently of their dubious relation to the Constitution.[23]

To allow internal improvements on general welfare, protectionist, pork barrel, or patronage grounds was simply bad public policy. According to Pierce, several disastrous consequences would result. First, it would be a short matter of time before nationally funded internal improvements included public education, public instruction, hospitals, sciences, arts, libraries, and "indeed everything appertaining to the internal welfare of the country." Second, the States' police powers and responsibilities would be displaced by national policies. Third, private enterprise would be paralyzed. Fourth, the legislative process would be perverted in the scramble for appropriations. Fifth, the national treasury would be exhausted, leaving taxpayers with a "heavy public debt, beyond the capacity of generations to discharge."[24]

Essentially rejecting the core of Clay's American System and outraging the factions benefiting from its financial windfalls, Pierce reaffirmed his party's 1852 platform when he announced, "From whatever point of view, therefore, the subject is regarded, whether as a question of express or implied power, the conclusion is the same, that Congress has no constitutional authority to carry on a system of internal improvements." It was this approach to domestic politics that stoked the controversy over the slavery issue, as his political opponents went on the offensive. Pierce's constitutionally solid policy not to expand the national government's role in the economy was met with every weapon in his opponents' political arsenal. Slavery proved to be a very effective weapon, indeed.

✠ IV ✠

The initial fugitive slave law (1793) allowed ingress and egress of slave owners into non-slave States and territories to retrieve their runaway slaves. Although the 1793 statute required slave owners to prove ownership before a local magistrate or federal court, many slave owners, or their agents, failed to do so and simply captured alleged fugitive slaves and returned them to their respective slave States. Several

Northern States reacted by passing personal liberty laws (which gave slaves and those alleged to be slaves certain due process rights in state courts) and strict anti-kidnapping laws (thereby heightening criminal penalties for those unlawfully pursuing slaves and alleged slaves).

In 1842 the US Supreme Court struck down the Northern States' accumulated statutory obstacles to the recovery of fugitive slaves, but also made the enforcement of Article IV's fugitive slave provision a federal, not state, public policy responsibility.[25] Following the court's decision, many Northern States used Justice Story's 1842 ruling that the States could not be forced to assist in the capture and return of fugitive slaves to pass new personal liberty laws. In response, Congress passed the fugitive slave law of 1850, a law that drove a bigger wedge between North and South, but nevertheless a law that Pierce was constitutionally obligated to enforce.

Article IV's fugitive slave clause is straightforward,[26] but predicated on an amicable relationship between Northern and Southern States, a relationship based upon a common understanding and acceptance of the rule of law. President Pierce was confronted with the increasingly volatile public policy nightmare of civility between Northern and Southern States being displaced by outright hostility. When Congress passed the 1850 Compromise it addressed the increasingly problematic enforcement of the Constitution's fugitive slave clause by passing a new Fugitive Slave Act. In its attempt to restore civility, Congress actually heightened interstate tensions.

Five years later, in 1855, the Massachusetts legislature passed "an Act to protect the Rights and Liberties of the People of the Commonwealth of Massachusetts." The provisions of these liberty laws statutorily prevented state personnel and facilities from being used to aid federal officials in the recapture of fugitive slaves. For example, section 15 stipulated, "Any sheriff, deputy sheriff, jailer, coroner, constable, or other officer of this Commonwealth, or the police of any city or town, or any district, county, city or town officer, or any officer or other member of the volunteer militia of this Commonwealth, who shall hereafter arrest . . . any person for the reason that he is claimed or adjudged to be a fugitive from service or labor, shall be punished by fine . . . and by imprisonment."[27] Such state responses to the 1850 Fugitive Slave Act amounted to interposition of national law. And unlike the crisis of the 1830s during which South Carolina interposed unconstitutional protective tariffs, the fugitive slave law was clearly constitutional. Neither as political partisan, as evidenced by the slavery plank of his party's platform, nor as chief executive, could Pierce countenance state obstructionism of constitutional obligations, at least not as long as the obstructing States remained members of the Union.

Pierce's point man on this most contentious issue of his presidency was US Attorney General Caleb Cushing.[28] Prior to his appointment as attorney general, Cushing was an associate justice of the Supreme Court of Massachusetts. Enduring the intensity of partisan Massachusetts politics, e.g., abolition, personal liberty laws, and the territorial issue, he had ample opportunities to observe challenges to and reaffirm his appreciation of the rule of law. This experience proved invaluable as he emphasized the quasi-judicial responsibilities of the office of attorney general. He functioned as the administration's de jure and de facto chief legal officer, second only to the president.[29]

In an opinion about the enforcement of the fugitive slave laws, sent to President Pierce on February 18, 1854, Cushing shaped the administration's policy towards the 1850 Fugitive Slave Act. His opinion rests upon the twin pillars of strict construction of the US Constitution and the congressional 1850 statute.

The opinion is in response to the request of a Mississippi slave owner, Mr. John B. Davis, for the assistance of the US government in recapturing his fugitive slave from the Choctaw Nation, located in territory west of the Mississippi River. The legal question focuses on the "right and the power of a citizen of the United States to reclaim fugitives from labor, who may be found in that portion of the territory of the United States, which lies without the limits of any State or any organized Territory."[30] This legal question implicates many of the burning issues of the 1850s, including status of slavery in the territories, the Missouri Compromise, the fugitive slave laws, personal liberty laws, and comity between the Northern and Southern States. Moreover, Cushing's opinion manifests the constraints that the rule of law placed on Pierce's options in dealing with these issues. A summary of Cushing's opinion makes this clear.

Article IV, section 1, of the US Constitution authorizes the US Congress to enact statutes to facilitate comity among the States by giving interstate effect to the "acts, records, and proceedings" of each state. The privileges and immunities clause of section 2, clause 1, prohibits the States from enacting laws that prevent citizens from other States from conducting interstate business. In today's parlance, these two sections established a free trade zone among the several States.

To further comity among the States, the Constitution mandates, "A person charged in any State with Treason, Felony, or other Crime, who shall flee from Justice, and be found in another State from which he fled, be delivered up, to be removed to the State having Jurisdiction of the Crime" (Article IV, section 2, clause 2). This clause covers fugitives from justice suspected of criminal and civil crimes. Section 2, clause 3, deals specifically with "persons held to service" in one state and escaping to another, covering both indentured servants and slaves.

Cushing encounters a problem, insofar as sections 1, 2, and 3 of Article IV make specific reference to States, but not to the territories of the United States. Mr. Davis's fugitive is not only in a territory, but in a portion of a territory under the jurisdiction of the Choctaw Nation. Cushing surmounts the constitutional technicality by articulating a model of federalism consistent with the 1852 Democratic Party Platform, i.e., a national government constitutionally limited to an evenhanded treatment of the States. Providing rationalization for the repeal of the Missouri Compromise in the Kansas-Nebraska Act of 1854, and anticipating the constraints of popular sovereignty in regard to slavery in the Dred Scott decision (1857), Cushing opines that the Congress lacks constitutional authority to exclude Southerners and their slave property from the territories.

Constitutional provisions dealing with full faith and credit, the territories, and fugitive slave laws *pari materia* (construed with reference to each other), support the Southern position.[31] Article IV, section 3, clause 2, confers on the Congress the "power to dispose of and make all needful Rules and Regulations respecting" the territories. However, such rules and regulations cannot constitutionally deprive citizens of the States or US citizens residing in a territory of their rights, including the constitutionally recognized right to own slave labor. As Cushing stated:

The whole truth seems to be, that, according to the principle of the

Constitution, the people of the States are self-constituent, and in them residues all theoretical sovereignty. Citizens of the United States, residing in the Territories, possess all the great rights which belong to them as citizens of their respective States. They compose the elements of a future sovereignty, existing on earth, which is, for the time being, the "property" of the Federal Union. Congress must, of necessity, have and exercise the power "to dispose of, and make rules and regulations respecting" this property of the Union, including among other things the power to subdivide unorganized Territory; in subordination of course to the guiding spirit of our political system, which is, to combine liberty with legality, to advance from the starting point of the agreed conditions and limits of the Constitution. The inhabitants of a Territory, whether commencing, pursuing, or consummating the successive stages of self-government, remain subject always to the restrictions of the Constitution. In fine, the letter of the Constitution wherever it is applicable, and the spirit of it in all things, is to be applied to the consideration of the rights of citizens of the United States in the Territories as well as in the States.[32]

With the territories being the common property of all the States, the US Congress is proscribed from conferring on the territorial government the prerogative to infringe upon the rights of citizens from any state, or US citizens from those States who have domiciled in a territory. Hence, the Missouri Compromise, territorial popular sovereignty, and treaties with Indian tribes cannot operate to "the detriment or diminution of the constitutional rights of the States" and their citizens.[33]

Cushing's opinion is as notable for what it does not say as for what it does. For example, it does not predicate the Union on a model of a national collectivity of individuals, as maintained by Lincoln and the Republican party. The Union is an organization of sovereign States, bound together by their common interests. Cushing's union is predicated on comity among the States. Because the States are sovereign, even extradition is subject to the rule of comity. The language of Article IV, section 2, clause 2, of the US Constitution is quite emphatic: "A person charged in any State with Treason, Felony, or other Crime, who shall flee from Justice, and be found in another State, shall on Demand of the executive Authority of the State from which he fled, be delivered up, to be removed to the State having Jurisdiction of the Crime."

Likewise, clause 3 stipulates, "No Person held to Service or Labour, . . . shall, in Consequence of any Law or Regulation therein, be discharged from such Service or Labour, but shall be delivered up on Claim of the Party to whom such Service or Labour may be due." Nevertheless, due to the sovereignty of the States, "extradition is not a matter of strict right, but of express convention, or otherwise of comity only."[34]

For Cushing and Pierce, the glue holding the Union together is comity among the States. In the absence of that comity, the Union is dissolved. Their model was a consensual union of States, based upon the common interests of it members. Strict enforcement of the rule of law was deemed to be essential in upholding the common interests of the States. Subjective, selective, and/or lax enforcement of the rule of law was in effect sectional favoritism, because the laws manifested what the States considered to be in their mutual interests. If the interests of one section substantially changed, then changes in the laws tying the Northern and Southern States together became imperative. If such changes in national laws, reflecting the mutual interests of all the States, were not forthcoming, or, in other words, if the common interests between the sections were not achievable within the context of a union of States, then a consensual union of States was no longer feasible. For Pierce the Union was a means to an end, i.e., the particularized interests of the States, whereas for Lincoln the Union was an end in itself.

◆ V ◆

President Pierce's only appointment to the US Supreme Court reveals much of his administration's commitment to the rule of law. When the nomination of Mr. Campbell went to the Senate for confirmation, he was denounced as a southern Alabamian fire-eater, a nullifier, and a secessionist.[35] So why would a native son of New Hampshire place on the nation's highest court a native son of south Alabama? And, assuming that Pierce was cognizant of Justice Campbell's politics and jurisprudence, what does this appointment to the US Supreme Court reveal about Pierce's approach to the sectional crisis vis-à-vis the rule of law? Justice Campbell's jurisprudence on the territorial question provides some answers.

The Pierce administration's evenhanded policy towards Southern States was tantamount to a high-wire balancing act. On the one hand was an emerging New England nationalism sustained by its increasing hostility to the culture and politics of the Southern States, and on the other a defensive Southern regionalism.[36] But the question remains, was Pierce's commitment to the rule of law a form of atavism doomed to failure in a changing America? And did this commitment to the rule of law stem from a lack of vision and leadership, for which he is to be criticized? Justice Campbell's[37] concurring opinion in the controversial *Dred Scott v. Sandford* case[38] is instructive. In hindsight the relevance of this case is obvious. By declaring unconstitutional the 1820 Missouri Compromise, the court poured salt into the sectional wounds, thereby precipitating the dismemberment of the Union four years later. But this outcome was not inevitable.

The legal issue addressed by Justice Campbell substantively deviates from the one articulated by President Jackson's appointee, Chief Justice Roger Taney. Chief Justice Taney asks, "The question is simply this: Can a negro, whose ancestors were imported into this country, and sold as slaves, become a member of the political community formed and brought into existence by the Constitution of the United States, and as such become entitled to all the rights, and privileges, and immunities guaranteed by that instrument to the citizen?" For Justice Campbell, the legal issue is:

> How much power may be exercised by the people of the Territory, before their admission to the Union, the courts of justice cannot decide. This must depend, for the most part, on political considerations, which cannot enter into the determination of a case of law or equity. I do not feel called upon to define the jurisdiction of the Congress. It is sufficient for the decision of this case to ascertain whether the residuary sovereignty of the States or people has been invaded by the 8th section of the [Missouri Compromise] act of 6th March 1820.[39]

Justice Campbell addresses the constitutionality of section 8, and avoids Chief Justice Taney's rhetorical obiter dictum about the history and status of Negro citizenship.

Although Chief Justice Taney and Justice Campbell arrived at the same conclusion, that the 8th section of the Missouri Compromise is unconstitutional, they arrived at that conclusion from different lines of reasoning. The chief justice's rationale is that even if a slave were located, with the intention of becoming a permanent resident, in a territory that prohibited slavery, the slave would remain a slave because Congress lacked the constitutional authority to allow a territory to prohibit slavery. Chief Justice Taney's reasoning controverted not only English common law precedent, but also international legal norms. Justice Campbell deviated from Chief Justice Taney in several important ways.

First, his opinion was consistent with both English common law and international law. A territorial government could constitutionally prohibit slavery, but the Congress lacked constitutional authority to mandate that the people of a territory do so. Affirming the legal practicality of popular sovereignty, he maintained that the legal status of the slave is contingent upon the law of the domicile where the slave permanently resides, not temporary residency: a new legal "status may be acquired by a change of domicile" by the owner and his slave property to a jurisdiction that prohibits slavery. Article IV, section 2, clause 3,[40] of the US Constitution is an implicit acknowledgment of this "ancient right," by stating that a temporary change of place does not affect the legal status of the slave.

Second, section 8 of the Missouri Compromise failed to pass constitutional muster because it violated the sovereign rights of those States that lie "north of thirty-six degrees and thirty minutes north latitude" to decide whether or not to prohibit slavery within their respective jurisdictions. Justice Campbell correctly maintained that the US government lacked constitutional authority to regulate slavery in the States, except for the foreign slave trade as it impacts the States. Any national power over slavery within the States "must therefore depend upon some condition of the Territories which distinguishes them from the States, and subjects them to a control more extended."

The congressional power of "a control more extended" rests upon Article IV, section 3, in which the Constitution grants to the Congress the "power to dispose and make all needful rules and regulations respecting the territory or other property belonging to the United States."[41] But these congressional powers over the territories is limited by the Tenth Amendment, which states: "The powers not delegated to the United States by the Constitution, nor prohibited by it to the States, are reserved to the States respectively, or to the people." The phrase "or to the people" includes the people in the territories. Because the Constitution does not contain a delegated power to the Congress to prohibit slavery in the States, it lacks the power to do so in the territories. Hence, section 8 of the Missouri Compromise is unconstitutional:

> This is a necessary consequence, resulting from the nature of the Federal Constitution, which is a federal compact among the States, establishing a limited Government, with powers delegated by the people of distinct and independent communities, who reserved to their State Governments, and to themselves, the powers they did not grant. This claim to impose a restriction upon the people of Missouri involved a denial of the constitutional relations between the people of the States and Congress, and confirmed a concurrent right for the latter, with their people, to constitute the social and political system of the new States. A successful maintenance of this claim would have altered the basis of the Constitution. The new States would have become members of a Union defined in part by the Constitution and in part by Congress.[42]

Justice Campbell, anticipating the approaching storm of the war between the States, admonishes the Congress not only for the unconstitutionality of the Missouri Compromise, but for the imprudent politics behind the law: "The Federal Government was constituted to exercise these powers [Article IV, section 3, clause 2] for the preservation of the States, respectively, and to secure to all their citizens the enjoyment of the rights which were not surrendered to the Federal Government. . . . No candid or rational man can hesitate to believe, that if the subject of the eighth section of the act of March, 1820, had never been introduced into Congress and made the basis of legislation, no interest common to the Union would have been seriously affected."[43]

The rule *of* law articulated by Justice Campbell was consistent with the Pierce administration's modus operandi and predicated upon four important tenets. First, originalism (interpreting the Constitution according to the framers' original intent) was the legitimate rule of construction for the Constitution, not the higher-law non-originalism of the Republican party. This is not to say that Pierce was hostile to higher law. Within the federal framework, according to Pierce, the respective States were the appropriate venues for working through higher-law principles. Second, the national government was constitutionally limited to the extent that the Whigs' and Republicans' domestic policy objectives of internal improvements and protective tariffs were not feasible. Third, the slavery issue was to be resolved by the people of the territories and the States. Even the Northwest Ordinance (1787), as noted by Justice Campbell, was a state initiative, stipulated by Virginia, and subsequently "ordained" by the US Congress.[44] And fourth, the Union was a compact among the several States and not a union of individuals. The compact theory of the Union is key to States' rights, democracy and the rule of law, to be distinguished from hypernationalism, elitism, and the rule *by* law.[45]

◄ VI ►

Pierce's affinity for the rule *of* law in contrast to the rule *by* law explains why such scorn has been heaped upon his presidency. Lincoln, had he complied with the rule of law and deferred to the US Constitution on the issues of secession, the writ of habeas corpus, the blockade of Southern ports, etc., may have presided over a realignment of the Union, but he also would have placed the rule of law on a constitutional pedestal that would have constrained subsequent presidents' quest for power. But Lincoln's claim to fame is not that he adhered to the rule of law, but that he had the audacity to disregard it.

Lincoln's unfortunate legacy is that he destroyed American federalism by creating a coercive, indissoluble Union. Consequently, the policy prerogatives of interposition, nullification, and secession are now placed beyond the grasp of the States. Nevertheless, the ever-expanding national government's powers continued to occupy the efforts of the courts in postbellum America. One example is Justice Sutherland's opinion in *Carter v. Carter Coal Company* (1936), a case that stemmed from Franklin Delano Roosevelt's expansion of national powers vis-à-vis the Tenth Amendment police powers of the States. Justice Sutherland articulates the anti-Lincoln premise that "the States were before the Constitution; and, consequently, their legislative powers antedated the Constitution." To concede otherwise is to begin a "forbidden journey" through which the national government takes over the "powers of the States" and the States "are so despoiled of their powers" that they are reduced to "little more than geographical subdivisions of the national domain." He continues, "It is safe to say that when the Constitution was under consideration, it had been thought that had any such danger lurked behind its plain words, it would never have been ratified."[46] Justice Sutherland's logic is just as applicable today, with the qualification that the "forbidden journey" has progressed to where the national government may be so "despoiled" of its powers that it will be reduced to "little more than geographical subdivisions" of the international domain.

Chapter IV

LIBERTY OR UNION

It is said that the right of secession, if conceded, makes our Government a mere rope of sand . . . better, far better, a rope of sand than the chains of iron, and shackles of steel.   US Sen. Judah P. Benjamin, Louisiana,
                                                                    February 4, 1861

***

We believe that the central challenge we face today is to ensure that globalization becomes a positive force for all the world's people.
                                    United Nations Millennium Declaration,
                                                    September 18, 2000

❧ I ❧

The European Union (EU) presents a twenty-first-century case study of how the rule of law is instrumental in the establishment of centralized authority. The EU centralizers are using the same tactics used by US elites to establish national supremacy over the States. Admittedly, the political, social, cultural, and economic dynamics are complex, and in various ways contribute to and/or detract from the establishment of centralized authority. Until recently Europe was much more decentralized than the nineteenth-century US. Nevertheless, three conclusions can be proffered at the outset. First, centralization must incrementally proceed, otherwise the nationalistic tendencies of the member States would derail the centralizing project. Second, incrementalism is highly dependent on the legal system to maintain the momentum of centralization and eventually complete the establishment of a legally sanctioned centralized authority. And third, the practicality of centralization rests upon a form of economic integration that makes the centralizing project politically, economically, and socially inevitable. Otherwise the centripetal forces would be overcome by the centrifugal cultural and social tendencies.

The historical precedent most useful to the EU framers is the transformation of US federalism into an increasingly unitary system of government. They have studied and taken into consideration the ups and downs of that transformation. They have learned from their American cousins, as contemporary global centralizers are learning from them. The overwhelming consensus of these centralizers on both sides of the Atlantic is their hostility to traditional notions of nation-based sovereignty.[1] This disdain should not be misconstrued as hostility towards government. To the contrary; the centralizers perceive traditional notions of sovereignty as obstacles to their policy agenda. It is not that they are opposed to government per se, but they are opposed to governments beyond their control.

For example, one useful EU centralizing tactic is the *principle of subsidiarity,* which is a highly subversive legal principle. Subsidiarity will facilitate the demise of national sovereignty in Europe, as applied by the European Court of Justice: "More than anything, subsidiarity thus serves as a critical viewpoint with which to constantly undermine the internal and external foundations of . . . State Sovereignty."[2] Full of interpretive opportunities similar to the US Constitution's Article VI supremacy clause, subsidiarity has been deceptively marketed as a guarantor of national sovereignty. That is why it has been credited with saving the Maastricht Treaty coalition from unraveling in 1991.[3] Nevertheless, the European Court of Justice has already made clear that its construction of the principle is one of centralization. The jurisprudential relevance of subsidiarity is substantial in overcoming national obstacles to international standards: "In international law subsidiarity can be understood to be a conceptual alternative to the comparatively empty and unhelpful idea of state [national] sovereignty."[4]

It is interesting how a process designed to limit the scope of the centralized authority is being utilized to undermine national sovereignty to the benefit of EU authority. This is accomplished by directing the operations of the EU not exclusively towards the nations, but towards the individuals composing the EU. The EU articulates the "principle of subsidiarity" as intended to ensure that decisions are taken as closely as possible to the citizen and that constant checks are made as to whether action at Community level is justified in the light of the possibilities available at national, regional or local level. Specifically, it is the principle whereby the Union does not take action (except in the areas which fall within its exclusive competence) unless it is more effective than action taken at national, regional or local level. It is closely bound up with the principles of proportionality and necessity, which require that any action by the Union should not go beyond what is necessary to achieve the objectives of the Treaty.[5]

Under Title III, article 1-11(3), the EU is authorized to go beyond its "exclusive competence" based upon the "principle of subsidiarity."[6] The nonexclusive competence includes the enforcement of the "values underlying humanism" directly on individuals throughout Europe:

The peoples of Europe, in creating an ever closer union among them, are resolved to share a peaceful future based on common values.

Conscious of its spiritual and moral heritage, the Union is founded on the indivisible, universal values of human dignity, freedom, equality and solidarity; it is based on the principles of democracy and the rule of law. It *places the individual at the heart of its activities* [emphasis added] by establishing the citizenship of the Union and by creating an area of freedom, security and justice. . . . To this end, it is necessary to strengthen the protection of fundamental rights in the light of changes in society, social progress and scientific and technological developments by making those rights more visible in a Charter.[7]

The EU's placement of the "individual at the heart of its activities" is comparable to Publius's placement of state citizens under the operation of the US government. Making the "operation of the government on the people in their individual capacities, in its ordinary and most essential proceedings, will . . . on the whole, designate it, in this relation, a national [centralized] government,"[8] the States notwithstanding. The same is true regarding "the principles of subsidiarity and proportionality" and the process of "creating an ever closer union." The former is instrumental in realizing the latter. The powers of the nations making up the EU are limited by establishing a direct link (i.e., Madison's "operation of the government") between EU citizens to EU authorities. The member nations are bypassed through the absorption of individuals into the larger European community, which in turn is governed by the EU.

The principle of subsidiarity is a means towards centralization by mandating that government actions throughout the EU comply with the "activities of the rest of society for the sake of the common good." Its companion principle, the principle of proportionality ("any action by the Community shall not go beyond what is necessary to achieve the objectives of this Treaty"),[9] makes the EU, and specifically the European Court of Justice, the ultimate decider of the greater common-good constraints with which all EU member States must comply. Lacking sovereign immunity, member States can be sued by other member States, institutions, or a natural or legal person.[10] The enforcement mechanism of EU policy is unambiguous EU judicial supremacy.

As was the case in the US experience, the constitutional status of secession is a key component of the union's viability when confronted with member-state resistance to centralization. The absence of a constitutional right to secede may indicate that the union is indissoluble, even when irreconcilable differences between central authority and its subunits reach a critical stage. But as was the case in the US, the implicit yet indisputable right to secede can be set aside by a determined jurisprudence. Thus, perhaps even an explicit right to secede may be thwarted by creative jurisprudence. The draft EU Constitution currently stipulates: "Any Member State may decide to withdraw from the Union in accordance with its own constitutional requirements."[11] This *decision to withdraw,* not to be confused with the *right to withdraw,* may have significant strings attached under EU judicial supremacy.

Thus, the authentic constitutional status of secession in a federal union of government reveals much about the nature of the ties that bind the member states together. This status affects whether the ties are primarily consensual or coercive, and commensurately the balance of power between central and national or state governments. As expressed in the 1861 statement by Sen. Judah P. Benjamin above, the ties binding the American States together may be "a rope of sand" or "chains of iron." A rope of sand may suffice in maintaining an enduring union if the member States share economic, cultural, and security interests. This was the CSA model.

Even in the absence of a centralized government with the legal authority to coercively maintain union membership, secession is the flipside of consent. However, when the economic, cultural, and/or security interests of the States diverge, and the consent of a member state (or States) to remain within the union is withdrawn, then compelling a state to remain in the union would be inconsistent with a union based upon the consent of all its national/state members, but not necessarily with the consent of some non-state members, e.g., cities and individuals, within the union.

In a consensual federal union, if substantial changes to the economic, cultural, and/or security needs of a member state develop, its membership in the union may be discontinued as its interests dictate. But once the centralized government assumes coercive enforcement powers to maintain the union, then the union becomes an end in itself, in contradistinction to a means to securing the interests of each of its member States. The nature of the union is then substantially changed from one designed to promote the collective interests of its member States, to one promoting the collective interests of a dominant coalition of Europeans who control the central authority. The option of member States to secede from, and thereby escape the control of, the central authority is the only way to guarantee a federal union that is based upon the consent of the member States.

The transformation of an EU predicated upon member States to one of the collective interests of Europeans can be facilitated through the principle of subsidiarity. If political units within the member States, such as cities, are more closely tied to EU authority than to national/state authority, then the national resistance to the EU authority can easily be undermined. For example, if Dublin were to successfully check, i.e., interpose, the authority of the Irish Parliament by appealing directly to the European Court of Justice, such an appeal would provide short-term autonomy for Dublin from the Irish Parliament. However, in the long term, Dublin and all of Ireland will eventually be subordinated to the control of the EU Parliament in Brussels. The end result is EU supremacy over both Dublin and Ireland.[12]

❧ II ❧

As evidenced by patterns in US jurisprudence, the transformation of a consensual union to a coerced one can occur within the rule of law. For more than three generations, the American Union was based upon the consent of all the States, but subsequently legitimated by the US Supreme Court to one based upon national coercion. This substantial modification to the democratic basis of American rule of law was made possible by the US military's destruction of the CSA, which in turn was sanctioned by the US Supreme Court when it declared secession to be unconstitutional in *Texas v. White* (1869).[13] It was not until that US Supreme Court decision that secession was written out of the American rule of law.

If the European Court of Justice (or the UN International Court of Justice,[14] for that matter) is to be precluded from establishing coercion as the basis of EU membership, the legal procedures used to convert the US Union from one of consent to coercion must be considered. According to Nobel laureate James M. Buchanan, writing about the EU Constitution, the constitutional status of secession is central to the discussion. Acknowledging the relevance of the "American experience" and the threat that the "central unit" presents to the sovereignty of its member States, he insisted, "There must also be some explicit acknowledgement, in the contract of establishment, of the rights of the citizens in the separate units to secede from union, upon agreement of some designated supra-majority within the seceding jurisdiction."[15] Buchanan perhaps does not give enough weight to the fact that even an explicit constitutional recognition of secession may be swept aside by a determined US Supreme Court, or the European Court of Justice, on the grounds that the central government has direct and shared jurisdiction over citizens. One possible scenario is that a member state may secede but citizens in a large metropolitan area within that state may decide to remain in the union. The subordinate relationship of the state/national courts to the union's courts makes such a scenario even more plausible.

In the US, the prerogatives of state high courts vis-à-vis the US Supreme Court and the constitutional status of state secession from the Union were merely implicit constitutional options, lacking the "explicit acknowledgement" recommended by Buchanan for the EU Constitution. Had there been explicit provisions recognizing parity between state and national high courts and a state's constitutional right to secede, US political development would have been substantially different. More specifically, if the right of secession had been made explicit in the text of the US Constitution, President Lincoln's war against the Confederacy and the Supreme Court case that sanctioned his policy towards secession, *Texas v. White,* would have been embarrassingly inconsistent with the American rule of law.[16] Because the US Constitution lacks an explicit provision allowing state secession from the Union, the US Supreme Court had the opportunity to articulate a new rule of law that explicitly denies the constitutional right of a state to secede from the Union and thereby effectively transformed the Union from one based upon the consent of the States to one of national coercion.[17]

From a public-policy perspective, the transformation of the American and European unions from associations based upon consent to ones based upon coercion is essentially the reallocation of power from the member States to centralized authority. The role of the American rule of law in this reallocation has been substantial.

Utilizing the "rule of law" in a wide range of policy areas, both economic and social, the US Supreme Court has been instrumental in transforming the Union from a consensual association of States to one increasingly relying on coercion.[18] The European Union is on track for a comparable transformation. The European Court of Justice will play a policy role similarly played by its US counterpart. It is highly probable that the expanding policy prerogatives of the EU will enhance the prospects of arbitrary applications of centralized power, with the European Court of Justice, its current deceptive obscurity notwithstanding, playing an increasingly important role in legitimizing the EU's expanding powers.[19]

Even in light of the recent EU Constitution ratification setbacks in France and the Netherlands,[20] the European Court of Justice is poised to keep the project on track. The court's initial obscurity is its strength and mimics the US Supreme Court's incremental rise to power in interesting ways.[21] For example, the European Court of Justice has been quietly facilitating European centralization and is determined to do more:

The [European] Court of Justice is the most underrated (and perhaps the most overworked) of the five major institutions of the EU. While the Commission and Council of Ministers attract most of the media and public attention, and become embroiled in the biggest political controversies, the Court has quietly gone about its business of clarifying the meaning of European law. Its activities have been critical to the progress of European integration, and its role just as significant as that of the Commission or Parliament, yet few Europeans know what it does.[22]

The same could be accurately written about the US Supreme Court. In the US, national supremacy was incrementally sanctioned by the Supreme Court with the acquiescence of the States through official approval, inattention, and/or failed resistance. National supremacy is now firmly ensconced in the American political process and jurisprudence. But most importantly it was the US Supreme Court's nullification of the States' implicit constitutional right to secession that dealt the deathblow to States' rights and a consensual federal union.

An outline of how the Supreme Court effected that transformation to national supremacy follows. Ironically, US national sovereignty is now facing challenges from international sources of law. Just as national supremacy triumphed over state sovereignty, US national sovereignty is being transformed by global developments.

❧ III ❧

Establishing national supremacy over the States would have been much more difficult without national judicial supremacy. Subordinating state supreme courts to the US Supreme Court precluded self-government in the public-policy areas where national policies were forced upon the States.

The rise of national judicial supremacy can be attributed to the cumulative effects of court rulings that have incorporated into American case law nationalistic legal norms. These norms are designed to augment nationalism by prohibiting state supreme courts from acting as courts of last resort to challenge what the state considers to be unconstitutional national policies.[23] The subordination of state supreme courts was accomplished by removing them as co-equal partners in resolving constitutional questions, especially questions involving the balance of power between the central and state governments. US Supreme Court justices resorted to the syllogism that (a) the Constitution mandates national policy uniformity, especially in the public-policy area of commerce; (b) public-policy uniformity and States' rights judicial federalism are incompatible; thus (c) States' rights judicial federalism is unconstitutional because it is contrary to national policy uniformity. The end result is the establishment of a hierarchical court system with the US Supreme Court atop the apex.[24]

Similarly, constructing a centralized Europe has been a work in progress towards policy uniformity across Europe. Nevertheless, the national policymaking prerogatives of, for example, the English parliament vis-à-vis the EU are ambiguous and analogous to the ambiguous American States' reserved powers vis-à-vis the US government's enumerated powers. In the United States the Supreme Court was pivotal in establishing national supremacy by gradually stripping the States of many of their reserved powers. European nation-states are destined for a similar fate as the EU continues down the road of integration and expansion.

The integration of new nation-states with greater economic, cultural, and political diversity will present more challenges to policy uniformity across the expanding EU, challenges mostly to be judicially resolved. The overarching, ambiguous jurisdiction of the European Court of Justice in the EU Constitution places member States in highly vulnerable positions regarding self-determination vis-à-vis EU policies. EU judicial supremacy over all other European courts is assured by the European Court of Justice's mandate to "ensure that in the interpretation and application of the [EU] Constitution the law is observed."[25]

Juridical "rule of law" developments similar to the US experience, if not apparent in the EU, are at least probable under the current institutional prerogatives of the European Court of Justice. The European Court of Justice and its Court of First Instance have important roles to play in transforming the formerly sovereign nations of Europe into a centralized European entity.[26] By providing the judicial safeguards ensuring that EU community law is superior to member-state law, i.e., EU policy interests trump national interests, the European Court of

Justice is well positioned to exercise judicial review over all member States and thereby impose EU policy mandates. This is a tremendous power, with opportunities to override the consent of significant segments of nationally based EU populations.

Although the American and European experiences are far from identical, there are parallels in the exercise of judicial power pertinent to both the US and EU highest courts. As manifested by the US experience, EU judicial power is substantially augmented if membership in the union is not contingent upon the ongoing consent of its members. However, if member States have the constitutionally reserved right to secede,[27] EU judges would be compelled to be more deferential towards member States's policy preferences. In a worst-case scenario, if the EU were to ignore important nationally based policy preferences, it could provoke secession as the avenue for the expression and maintenance of nation-based popular control and consent within the territorial limits of the member States.

Moreover, it should not be assumed that the European Court of Justice would impartially adjudicate power struggles between the union and its member states. As evidenced by US Supreme Court case law on judicial federalism and state secession, the US Supreme Court served as an agent of partisan politics and its nationalistic ambitions. This is why European Court of Justice supremacy over all the member States courts is so problematical.

Indeed, an overview of US Supreme Court case law makes evident that the court was institutionally determined to transfer the locus of sovereignty from the States to the US government.[28] Due to national judicial supremacy, the US Supreme Court could effectively incorporate into the American rule of law a version of centralization that ultimately excluded secession as a component of States' rights. The relevant case law behind these developments reveals a jurisprudence that EU member States should be cognizant of if they value a viable federalism and a union grounded upon the consent of member States, i.e., a viable democracy.

⚔ IV ⚓

Since the Union's origins in 1789, the fundamental challenge of

American case law has been the balance of power between national and state governments. Consider Tocqueville's perspective of the imbalance of power between the States and national government in the 1830s:

> The first difficulty Americans had to face was how to divide sovereignty so that the various states of the Union continued to govern themselves in everything to do with internal prosperity but so that the whole nation, represented by the Union, should still be a unit and should provide for all general needs. That was a complicated question and hard to resolve. . . . The duties and rights of the federal government were simple and easy to define because the Union had been formed with the object of providing for certain great general needs. But the rights and duties of the governments of the states were many and complicated, for such a government was involved in all the details of social life. Therefore the attributes of the federal government were carefully defined, and it was declared that everything not contained within that definition returned to the jurisdiction of state governments. Hence state authority remained the rule and the federal government the exception.[29]

Even though "the rights and duties of the governments of the states [are] many and complicated" and, indeed, have been substantially expanded since Tocqueville's analysis, those of the federal government have grown beyond the framers' worst fears. Over time, state restrictions on the expansion of national power proved to be ineffective, in large part because the US Supreme Court failed to recognize States as sovereign entities.

This "first difficulty Americans had to face" was acknowledged by Publius's *imperium in imperio*. When Publius charged that the Anti-Federalists aimed at "things repugnant and irreconcilable; at an augmentation of federal [i.e., national] authority without a diminution of State authority; a sovereignty in the Union and complete independence in the members," he was being somewhat disingenuous. The use of a canard to place one's political opponents on the defensive may be an effective rhetorical trick, but it is plain that the States did not seek to retain "complete independence" within the Union, as is amply evidenced by the delegation of certain powers to national authority (e.g., Article 1, section 8) and limitations to state authority (Article 1, section 10). The States were not concerned with *imperium in imperio* per se, but with the constitutional ambiguity surrounding *imperium.* In other words, how were the States (the principals) to keep the central government (their agent) from usurping control over their reserved powers?

Sovereignty was not divided in 1789. The States collectively delegated to the national government certain responsibilities and the attendant powers to fulfill those responsibilities, but not their respective sovereignties. Point to the document, process, or constitutional provision through which the States conceded sovereignty to the national government. There is none, with the important exception of fraudulent American case law.

The language and structure of the US Constitution manifest where sovereignty resides, as does the ratification record. Most significantly, there is neither explicit nor implicit evidence that the States transferred their sovereignty to the national government. According to common law, as understood at the time of the Constitution's ratification, an implicit transfer of state sovereignty to the national government was untenable. It is worth repeating St. George Tucker's[30] admonition: "The powers delegated to the federal government being all positive, and enumerated according to the ordinary rules of construction, whatever is not enumerated is retained; for expressum facit tacere tacitum [that which is expressed makes that which is implied to cease] is a maxim in all cases of construction: it is likewise a maxim of political law, that sovereign states cannot be deprived of any of their rights by implication; nor in any manner whatever by their own voluntary consent, or by submission to a conqueror."[31]

Moreover, there is ample evidence that each state retained its ultimate sovereignty in the event of an irreconcilable conflict with the other States organized into a union. As evidenced by Article V of the US Constitution (the amendment article), Article III, section 3 ("treason against the United States, shall consist only in levying War against *them*" [emphasis added]), Article VII ("the ratification of nine States"), and the Eleventh Amendment ("one of these United States"), the States are the parts of the constitutional national compact; the States are the principals and the national government their agent. This explains why three States conditionally acceded to the Union, thereby reserving the constitutional option to secede.[32] Exercising such an option is the prerogative of sovereign authority, a prerogative acknowledged by the other States when they accepted conditional ratification. Conditional ratification and its acceptance by the other States stemmed from the American political culture of the late eighteenth-century, which was predominantly anti-centralization. That is why central government's powers are constitutionally constrained by a written document, checks and balances, separation of powers, the bill of rights, the amendment process, and the absence of explicit national supremacy.

The original Article VI supremacy clause does not support national sovereignty. The record is clear that Chief Justice Marshall's commentary on Article VI's supremacy clause is disingenuous and a guise to read into the US Constitution national supremacy and read out of it state sovereignty. The Article VI stipulations that "the Constitution, and the Laws of the United States which shall be made in Pursuance thereof; and all Treaties made, or which shall be made, under the Authority of the United States, shall be the supreme Law of the Land; *and the Judges in every State shall be bound thereby* [emphasis added], any Thing in the Constitution or Laws of any State to the Contrary notwithstanding" are rules of construction for state judges. State judges were to decide what is and is not pursuant to the Constitution. As stated by the American Blackstone, St. George Tucker, the States retained their respective sovereignties.

This raises a clear question. With all these checks on centralized power, how did the Supreme Court alter the American constitutional order to the point where the States were stripped of their individual sovereignty? It is also important to consider in what manner and to what extent nationalism is susceptible to a similar fate at the hands of transnational levels of government such as the UN. The answers are to be found in the ingenious judicial substitution of the American rule *of* law with the rule *by* law.

❧   V   ❧

Once the US Supreme Court placed itself at the apex of the American court system, state judges accepted US Supreme Court case-law precedents as controlling. Accordingly, when state judges incorporated into state case law the nationalistic precedents established by the US Supreme Court, the States were inadvertently conceding important aspects of state sovereignty. This is partially explained by the fact that some States experienced a boon to their political fortunes when national power was augmented.[33]

The pillars of nationalism are the legislative, executive, and judicial branches. These branches of government mark the actual and potential policy instruments of state coalitions, organized through the mechanisms of political parties. In other words, nineteenth-century power struggles between the Union and States (e.g., tariffs, admission of new States, internal improvements, slavery, etc.) were essentially contests of one coalition of States against another. The coalition that successfully implemented its policy objectives did so by controlling some, if not all, of the US government. Compromise on an issue was due to a sort of balance of power among state coalitions. Admittedly, the alignments among the States were very fluid and therefore resolvable without tearing the Union to pieces, with the exception of the war between the States, from 1861 to 1865.

That crisis resulted when the seceded Southern States capitulated to Northern and Western States all the institutions of the US government. Anticipating their declining ability to effect compromise due to the emergence of a sectionalized Republican party, the Southern States seceded from the Union. They established their own confederated union, with additional checks and balances designed to more securely protect the policy prerogatives of some States vis-à-vis other States in the CSA.[34] Nevertheless, those States that remained in the old Union, not wanting to relinquish their policy dominance over the Southern States, utilized their control of the national government to militarily maintain control over the breakaway Southern States. Lincoln personified the national imperium.[35] He was, essentially, the agent acting on behalf of the coalition of Northern and Western States. By 1860, Southerners realized that the election of Lincoln was symptomatic of a Union already irreversibly divided. It was not the man Lincoln that was so problematical but the coalition of States behind the man, and his regionally based Republican party.

The courts, following "the economic activity that underlay and drove politics,"[36] determined which constitutional model would prevail, the

States' rights or the nationalistic model. But nationalism is essentially a phenomenon of States acting in unison towards some common goal or goals. Would it be feasible for the national government to pursue a policy objective that a majority of the States adamantly opposed? For example, could Lincoln have succeeded in subjugating the independent Confederacy (the established agent of a coalition of Southern States' policy interests) without the support of Northern States? Or, more specifically, with the support of a Northern numerical majority, but without the support of a majority of Northern States, would Lincoln's policies to destroy the CSA have prevailed?

Divided sovereignty is commensurate with the various and complex political fault lines separating the States, with the varying forms of nationalism being the manifestations of those fault lines. North against South means Northern States against Southern States. Hence, the term "American Civil War" is overly simplistic. Much more accurate is the idea of a war between state coalitions, acting through their respective US and CSA unions.

This is not to say that influential political leaders did not favor a unitary, in contradistinction to a federal, form of government. There have been notable successes towards that transition by influential state leaders who gained the national stage to promote their state's interests. For example, economic interests were critical in the success of Chief Justice Marshall's jurisprudence "used to justify every manner of federal intrusion on the rights of the states." The evolution of the country's economic activity was anything but static. Monetization of society, demographic changes, developments in manufacturing, and even an information revolution profoundly affected public-policy preferences regarding internal improvements, protective tariffs, and slavery. As policy preferences changed, so too did political activists' preferences for either States' rights or nationalism. Depending upon which model was most conducive to one's policy objectives, that model was rhetorically defended against one's political opponents. According to Forrest McDonald, this helps to explain how early in his career Daniel Webster was a hardcore States' rights advocate and John C. Calhoun a nationalist.[37]

Even though the original Constitution was overwhelmingly inclined towards States' rights, as the nation developed, factions emerged that favored a much stronger national government.

Two regionally based groups in particular fit that description. Western States (and territories) sought internal improvements, such as roads, canals, and river dredging, to be funded by the US government, which is to say at the expense of the taxpayers from other States, and Northern States, reflecting the policy preferences of their manufacturers and capitalists, sought US government protection from foreign competition through the use of protective tariffs and sought the financial stability that a reconstituted, revitalized, and effectively managed Bank of the United States could provide.[38] The economies of the Southern States linked their interests to the status quo, i.e., a limited national government.

By late 1860 and early 1861, these groups' respective preferences jelled, if not hardened. McDonald writes, "Leaders on both sides of the conflict were strangely loath to admit that it had anything to do with slavery. Abraham Lincoln insisted at the outset that the war was being fought solely to preserve the Union as he conceived the Union—namely, as one among the American people, not among the states."[39] The reason for Lincoln's stance was that the old Union, the one with the States as its constituent parts, was an obstacle to the policy pursuits of the Republican party.

This does not mean that in April of 1861 Lincoln proceeded to destroy the CSA and intentionally drench American soil with the blood of Yankees and Confederates. Is it more probable that he was a very poor prognosticator of events? Because his political brokering misfired, he covered his misdeeds with the rhetoric of emancipation and charity towards all.[40]

From a public-policy perspective, States' rights passed through the war crucible seemingly intact, but not from a jurisprudential perspective. The military events of 1861-65 set the stage for the substance of States' rights prerogatives to be thereafter diverted away from the States to the national government. Developments such as Reconstruction, national fiscal policy, and US Supreme Court jurisprudence did not alter state and national relations in one fell swoop but incrementally, so that by the time of Pres. Lyndon B. Johnson's Great Society, "the vestiges of States' rights that remained were obliterated."[41]

As the US Supreme Court bestowed its imprimatur on national power, there emerged an American rule of law that not only curtailed

States' rights but sewed nationalism into the warp and woof of American life. Whether the growth of national power is exclusive of or concurrent with States' rights, the States as sovereign entities have correspondingly less power vis-à-vis the national government. This is especially true since the national government determines the extent of its powers, States' rights notwithstanding. In other words, the national agent has been transformed into the principal, and the States as principals into the agents of national economic and social-policy objectives.

How did this reversal of roles occur? When the constitutional tie that ultimately binds the union of States together was switched from consent to coercion, the nature of the union was fundamentally altered. The individual States had to be constitutionally stripped of sovereignty and its locus shifted to the central authority. This is not to say that the States were unwilling to concede elements of state sovereignty when offered national public-policy goodies. But those goodies (e.g., internal improvements, protectionism, a national bank) had costs attached. Even though the balance between state police and national commerce powers seemed to be somewhat settled in 1847 when Chief Justice Roger Brooke Taney articulated a state's police powers as "the power to govern men and things within the limits of its own dominion,"[42] the realm of the national government's policy prerogatives was expanding before the ink in his opinion was dry.

That expansion was in large measure beneficial to those States that had vested interests in the governmental support and protection of industrialization.[43] Consequently, the clashing interests of an increasingly industrialized North and an agrarian South were affecting all aspects of American politics. Nevertheless, as long as consent was the basis of membership in the Union, the expansion of national power was in accord with state sovereignty. When Southern States exercised an option of sovereignty and seceded from the Union, beginning with South Carolina on December 20, 1860, the American constitutional landscape began to develop into a Union predicated upon coercion. The watershed case marking the legal end of the consensual Union is the postbellum US Supreme Court case *Texas v. White*. This 1869 case displaced consent and constitutionalized coercion as the epoxy of the Union.[44]

The causal links between US economic and juridical developments indicate that European economic integration will similarly impact the development of EU case law and that an EU version of *Texas v. White* is highly probable. And in time, it is also probable that economic globalization will have a corresponding impact on the United Nations' World Court case law, tending to morph regional governing unions into globally based ones.

❧ VI ❧

The underlying constitutional issue in *Texas v. White* is whether sovereignty is state or nation based. This issue is as old as the Constitution, but dissimilar from previous constitutional questions about national supremacy, judicial review, state nullification, and interposition, all of which were in the context of the States' voluntary memberships in the Union. The States acknowledged that membership in the Union curtailed a good portion of their public-policy options, but the curtailment was consensual insofar as the States voluntarily remained in the Union. This is an important qualification. National policies most anathema to a state's interests are peculiarly consensual as long as a state's membership in the Union is voluntary. Seceding from the Union would effectively arrest unwanted national policies within the jurisdiction of the seceding state or States.[45] However, if membership in the Union is coercively maintained against the preference of a would-be independent State, then the basis of national policies within the jurisdiction of the state is coercive.[46]

In *Texas v. White*, Chief Justice Salmon P. Chase maintained, "The Constitution, in all its provisions, looks to an indestructible Union, composed of indestructible States."[47] Chase's cliché hinges on a theory destructive of a Union based upon reflection and choice, i.e., consent. The indestructible Union and its subsequent incorporation into American case law are substantial deviations from the feeble Union that predated the policies of the Lincoln administration. More than a matter of constitutional law, the "feeble Union" was a product of American culture. As noted by Tocqueville,

The federal government therefore, in spite of the efforts of its founders, is, as I have said before, one of such naturally feeble sort that it requires, more than any other, the free support of the governed in order to survive. . . . If today the sovereignty of the Union was to come into conflict with one of the states, one can readily foresee that it would not succumb; I even doubt whether such a struggle would ever be seriously undertaken. Each time that determined resistance has been offered to the federal government, it has yielded. Experience has proven that up till now, when a state has been obstinately determined on anything and demanded it resolutely, it has never failed to get it; and when it has flatly refused to act, it has been allowed to refuse.[48]

Obviously a far different Union emerged from the war than the one Tocqueville portrayed. This is not to say that States' rights were finished circa 1865. But it is to say that the groundwork, with constitutional sanction, had been laid for a dominant national government presiding over a union of subservient States. Chase's jurisprudence makes this quite evident.

In order to grasp *Texas v. White*'s long-term significance, attention must be refocused on a concept of American jurisprudence that the court did its best to bury in 1869. The concept is political obligation as manifested in what constitutes a treasonable offense in a federal system.

State secession from the Union is in a class by itself and should not be equated with the reams of sedition statutes that clutter US and state codes. Sedition may be treasonable because it is essentially insurrection, relying on unlawful (i.e., criminal) means to reach a political objective. But Southern secession was predicated on the established constitutional grounds that a state may withdraw its political obligation from the union of States as organized and managed under the United States government.

A state's withdrawal from the Union was constitutional if certain procedural guidelines were adhered to. The guidelines were intended to ensure that secession was compatible with the republican principle of grounding government in the consent of the governed, and the state, not the nation, was the unit responsible for measuring consent. If "treason is declared to consist *only in levying war against the United States, or in adhering to their enemies, giving them aid and comfort*"[49] [emphasis added], Confederate actions in the war were not treasonable because they ceased to be US citizens as a consequence of secession.

Moreover, if individuals within a particular state violated republican principles in the course of secession, such actions would not constitute treason against the US. "Similar acts committed against the laws or government of a particular state, are punishable according to the laws of that state, but do not amount to treason against the United States."[50]

Was (is) state secession from the Union treasonable? In *Texas v. White* the court answered with a qualified yes. Its answer had to be qualified because of the constitutional safeguards against politically motivated convictions for treason.[51] The Constitution explicitly stipulates: "Treason against the United States, shall consist only in levying War against them, or in adhering to their Enemies, giving them Aid and Comfort. No Person shall be convicted of Treason unless on the Testimony of two Witnesses to the same overt Act, or on Confession in open Court."[52] If the court were to jurisprudentially equate secession with treason, then the state secessionist leaders, acting in their respective official state capacities, would have had to be charged accordingly and afforded their criminal procedural rights. Not only would the trials be numerous, but many of the venues would have been in the former Confederacy. Local juries would have been very unsympathetic to treason convictions.

To surmount this difficulty, Chief Justice Chase devised a jurisprudence that sanctioned the Republican party's war policies and a US government grounded in coercion. He resorted to concocting an American common-law definition of treason capable of sustaining the Union at all costs, especially when the Union is confronted with States' attempts to withdraw their political obligation. The Union was transformed from a voluntary association of States to an indestructible Union, the consent of the States notwithstanding. To achieve the objective of an "indestructible Union," *Texas v. White* resorted to an unprecedented disdain for popular control within the context of American federalism. In order to criminalize state secession, the court had to designate state conventions and legislatures into the *locus criminis* (the place where a crime was committed) whenever they exercised the constitutional right to secede.

As is the case with all the States of the CSA, there is no evidence of a crime in the procedures used by Texas to secede. Consistent with state secession from the British Empire in 1776[53] and the contemporary actions of her sister seceding States in 1860-61, the Texas convention approved the following ordinance:

> To dissolve the Union between the State of Texas and the other States united under the Compact styled "The Constitution of the United States of America."

> WHEREAS, the Federal Government has failed to accomplish the purposes of the compact of the union between these States, in giving protection either to the persons of our people upon an exposed frontier, or to the property of our citizens, and

> WHEREAS, the action of the Northern States of the Union is violative of the compact between the States and the guarantees of the Constitution; and,

> WHEREAS, the recent developments in Federal affairs make it evident that the power of the Federal Government is sought to be made a weapon with which to strike down the interests and property of the people of Texas, and her sister slave-holding States instead of permitting it to be, as was intended, our shield against outrage and aggression; THEREFORE,

> SECTION 1. We, the people of the State of Texas, by delegates in convention assembled, do declare and ordain that the ordinance adopted by our convention of delegates on the 4th day of July, A. D. 1845, and afterwards ratified by us, under which the Republic of Texas was admitted into the Union with other States, and became a party to the compact styled "The Constitution of the United States of America," be, and is hereby, repealed and annulled.[54]

Nevertheless, Chief Justice Chase maintained that the actions taken by the people of Texas on the path to secession and membership in the Confederate States of America were the actions of an insurgent legislature engaged in rebellion.[55] Chase's insurgency and rebellion axioms are merely assertions that must be accepted as articles of faith and not fundamental principles of American constitutionalism arrived at through thoughtful and reasoned legal argumentation.

Chief Justice Chase conceded, "Acting upon the theory that the rights of a State under the Constitution might be renounced, and her obligations thrown off at pleasure, Texas undertook to sever the bond thus formed [when Texas was admitted into the Union as a state on December 27, 1845], and to break up her constitutional relations with the United States. . . . In all respects, so far as the object could be accomplished by ordinances of the conventions, by acts of the legislature, and by votes of the citizens, the relations of Texas to the Union were broken up, and new relations to a new government were established for them."[56] But he concluded that Texas's secession and subsequent membership in the CSA were constitutionally impermissible because the "perfect Union" is indissoluble.[57] It was Texas's assault on the "perfect Union" that constituted the crime and criminalized secession. In other words, Texans in support of secession were criminals and as criminals took over the government of Texas. According to this logic, Texas ceased to have a republican form of government and needed to be rescued by the US Army.

❧ VII ❧

Was Texas's secession from the Union criminal and were Texans criminals? In order to legitimize the Northern States' war of aggression against the CSA, Chief Justice Chase needed to resort to some very creative jurisprudence. He argued that there is no jurisprudential precedent for state secession; because the court never had to adjudicate the constitutionality of it there was no binding precedent. The closest the court came to the issue was in the 1849 *Luther v. Borden*[58] case, which Chase relied on for his "republican form of government guaranty clause" precedent.

His reliance on the "guaranty clause" as articulated in that case is disingenuous. Chase had to concoct a constitutional rationale for (a) Reconstruction policies as presidential and congressional prerogatives, (b) denoting the actions of state secessionists as criminal and their subsequent official acts as members of the Confederacy as non-enforceable, and (c) the displacement of consent by coercion as the glue of the Union. Section 4 of Article IV was his most practical constitutional hook, even though it breaks under the weight of unbiased scrutiny.

First, Article IV, section 4, stipulated, "The United States shall guarantee to every State *in this Union* [emphasis added] a Republican Form of Government." But Chase ignored the obvious, that Texas ceased to be in the Union and therefore the guaranty clause ceased to be operative in Texas. Second, section 4 continues: "and shall protect each of them against Invasion." However, the only invading forces were those of the Union Army. And third, section 4 continues "and on the Application of the Legislature, or of the Executive . . . against domestic Violence." No such application was forthcoming from Texas, because from the Texan perspective there was no domestic violence that necessitated US government intervention.

Chase ruled: "In the exercise of the power conferred by the guaranty clause, as in the exercise of every other constitutional power, a discretion in the choice of means is necessarily allowed. It is essential only that the means be necessary and proper for carrying into execution the power conferred, through the restoration of the State to its constitutional relations, under a republican form of government, and that no acts be done, and no authority exerted, which is either prohibited or unsanctioned by the Constitution."[59] According to Chase, Lincoln's war and the Republican party's reconstruction policies in Texas (and the rest of the subjugated Confederacy) were constitutional because legitimate republican government had been displaced by non-republican government. Neither the facts nor case law support his findings. Consider his definition of "State" within the context of the US Constitution: "A State, in the ordinary sense of the Constitution, is a political community of free citizens occupying a territory of defined boundaries, and organized under a government sanctioned and established by *the consent of the governed* [emphasis added]. It is the union of such States, under a common constitution, which forms the distinct and greater political unit, which that Constitution designates as the United States, and makes of the people and the States which compose it one people and one country."[60]

The operational phrase is "the consent of the governed." The definition holds together as long as the state government is grounded in the consent of the governed. The United States is the collective government of States "with defined boundaries, and organized . . . and established by the consent of the governed" within the respective States. Chase overlooks the fact that logic dictates that for the State of Texas to remain within the Union, when the "free citizens" of Texas demanded secession, would have illegitimatized the state government. It would have ceased to be a republican form of government.

Relying on *Luther v. Borden,* Chase maintained that it is the responsibility of the Congress to determine whether or not a state government is republican. According to his twisted logic, the fact that Texas failed to apply for the assistance of the national government in securing a republican form of government during its secession is of greater significance than if she had. This failure on the part of Texas is of greater weight vis-à-vis the guaranty clause, because it is evidence that she had been "deprived of all rightful government, by revolutionary violence."[61]

But according to standards previously established by Supreme Court case law, Texas did have a republican form of government when and after it seceded from the Union. Chief Justice Taney ruled under Article IV, section 4:

> It rests with Congress to decide what government is the established one in a State . . . and whether it is republican or not. And when the senators and representatives of a State are admitted into the councils of the Union, the authority of the government under which they are appointed, as well as its republican character, is recognized by the proper constitutional authority. And its decision is binding on every other department of the government, and could not be questioned in a judicial tribunal.[62]

Significantly, Texas senators and congressmen voluntarily resigned from their respective seats in the US Senate and House, and were not disqualified because "the authority of the government under which they [were] appointed" was determined by the Congress to be non-republican. US Senator Wigfall (TX) adumbrated the same to his Senate colleagues on March 7, 1861, several weeks after Texas officially seceded. After acknowledging that South Carolina, Georgia, Florida, Alabama, Texas, and Louisiana had revoked the powers delegated to the US government,[63] he admonished his Northern colleagues:

> You must withdraw your troops; take your flag out of our country; allow us the right of self-government; enter into treaties with us afterwards or

not, as you see fit; but you must do that or make up your minds to have war—war in its sternest aspect, and with all its consequences. You must make no attempt to levy tribute upon us. . . . Mr. President, I have tried to explain, several times, the position which I occupy. I am not officially informed that the State which I represent has abolished the office of United States Senator. When I am so advised officially, I shall file at your desk that information; and then if, after being so informed, you shall continue to call my name, I will answer, probably if it suits my convenience.[64]

By the US Supreme Court's own legal standards, Texas, as were all the States of the CSA, was led out of the Union and into the Confederacy by a republican government, otherwise Senator Wigfall would have been disqualified from holding his US Senate seat. Furthermore, as evidenced by Wigfall's remarks on the floor of the US Senate, his continued participation in Senate business was at the discretion of Texas, because Texas met the criteria of a republican form of government. Such was certainly the official position of Texas, as manifested in its convention, which maintained that "all political power is inherent in the people, and all free governments are founded on their authority, and instituted for their benefit; and they have, at all times, the inalienable right to alter, reform or abolish their form of government, in such manner as they may think expedient."[65]

All the procedural safeguards taken by Texas notwithstanding, Chief Justice Chase asserted that the purpose of Texas's secession and subsequent defensive posture towards the Union was to avoid its obligations to the national government and to wage war against the United States to achieve that end.[66] Accordingly, these actions were treasonable and left Texas without a legitimate government. Hence, under the guaranty clause, the national government could do whatever it deemed necessary and proper to restore Texas to its constitutional relations to the United States.[67] The underlying premise of Chase's circular reasoning is that whether or not a state has a republican form of government is contingent upon its compliance with US government policies.

This explains why many of Texas's official acts between 1861 and 1865 were declared by the court to be valid, such as those "necessary to peace and good order among citizens, such for example, as acts sanctioning and protecting marriage and the domestic relations, governing the course of descents, regulating the conveyances and transfer of property, real and personal, and providing remedies for injuries to person and estate, and other similar acts, which would be valid if emanating from a lawful government." Those that were invalid included all "acts in furtherance or support of rebellion against the United States, or intended to defeat the just rights of citizens, and other acts of like nature." The latter type was constitutionally invalid because it was, "within the express definition of the Constitution, treasonable."[68]

According to longstanding legal principles, Chase's assertion that Texas engaged in treason was itself treasonable against the lawful government of Texas. According to St. George Tucker,

> Were an armed multitude, arrayed in order of battle, to enter and burn the city of Richmond, destroy all the public records of the state, and commit every other possible outrage, aggravated with every atrocious circumstance imaginable, if their intention in so doing, should neither be to subvert the constitution of the United States, nor effect any object in relation to the authority of the federal government, such conduct, though, in the strictest sense it might amount to actual levying war, would only amount to treason against the state of Virginia, but could never be treason against the United States. For treason against the latter, shall consist only in levying war against THEM, &c. Nor can it be pretended that the levying war against the authority of any individual state, within the same, would be levying war against the United States in any case; except in case of insurrection or rebellion, such state should make application to the United States for such aid as the constitution guarantees to them in such cases: after which if the opposition should extend to the authority of the United States, it seems that the treason would also extend to them.[69]

The scenario used by Tucker to exemplify what constitutes treason against the United States is in stark contrast to the relatively orderly procedures used by Texas to withdraw from the Union and accede to the CSA. If Tucker's hypothetical scenario does not constitute treason against the United States, how could the 1861 actions by Texas do so?

With Texas's secession and its "rebellion against the United States" declared to be the act of an "insurgent government," the United States government was authorized to suppress the rebellion and restore to

Texas a state government with "peaceful" (i.e., subservient) relations to the United States. Elevating nationalist ideology to constitutional status, Chief Justice Chase posited, "What can be indissoluble if a perpetual Union, made more perfect, is not?"[70]

From this premise, Chief Justice Chase leads American jurisprudence away from its historical roots of popular control and consent within the context of traditional States' rights federalism and into the implacable realm of empire:

> The Constitution, in all its provisions, looks to an indestructible Union, composed of indestructible States. When, therefore, Texas became one of the United States, she entered into an indissoluble relation. All the obligations of perpetual union, and all the guarantees of republican government in the Union, attached at once to the State. The act which consummated her admission into the Union was something more than a compact; it was the incorporation of a new member into the political body. And it was final. The union between Texas and the other States was as complete, as perpetual, and as indissoluble as the union between the original States. There was no place for reconsideration, or revocation, except through revolution, or through the consent of the States.[71]

By the stroke of his pen, the original thirteen and all the subsequently admitted States are, for all intents and purposes, merged into one consolidated domain.[72] And because a state's incorporation into the Union is irreversible, secession was the criminal action of rebels lacking legal authority to so act. "If this were otherwise, the State must have become foreign, and her citizens foreigners. The war must have ceased to be a war for the suppression of rebellion, and must have become a war for conquest and subjugation."[73]

In his dissenting opinion, Justice Grier was more blunt:

> The ordinance of secession was adopted by the convention on the 18th of February, 1861; submitted to a vote of the people, and ratified by an overwhelming majority. I admit that this was a very ill-advised measure. Still it was the sovereign act of a sovereign State, and the verdict on the trial of this question, "by battle," as to her right to secede, has been against her.[74]

Justice Grier's conclusion that the war between the States was a war of conquest was unpalatable to Chief Justice Chase. Chase realized that to concede as much was to make Washington, DC, the *locus criminis* and Mr. Lincoln an acknowledged criminal.

But this is precisely how Southerners viewed the war. The war waged against the Confederacy "disregards all constitutional restrictions, and finds its pabulum in the proud and avaricious desire to set up a great government which will extend its power to the ends of the earth, and enable the merchant and the manufacturer of the North to make money out of all nations, kindreds and tongues; and this money to be made by so regulating commerce with the States, that the agricultural States be made tributary to the commercial and manufacturing States," a Virginia Masonic lodge stated. "From such a Union we believe it was the solemn duty of our State to withdraw; and since her withdrawal we have abundant evidence that we were right."[75]

❧ VIII ❧

The locus of sovereignty was originally in the States. Furthermore, the formation of the American Union was based upon the collective consent of all the States, as evidenced by the drafting, ratification, and text of the US Constitution. But once a State acceded to the Union, did it forfeit its right of consent in regard to its continued membership in the Union? According to the US Supreme Court, the answer is a qualified yes. It is qualified in the sense that a state could petition the Union to acquiesce in its withdrawal from the Union, but such acquiescence is contingent upon the consent of the other States (Chief Justice Chase does not stipulate if that consent has to be unanimous). And in the absence of Union acquiescence to the secession of a state (or States), the remaining option is revolution.

Hence, a state determined to secede is nailed to the Union until or unless it procures the consent of the other States or successfully revolts. For the would-be independent state, this model of federalism approximates what Hamilton described as one predicated upon accident and force,[76] and consistent with the rule of law only insofar as it is sanctioned by the tribunal "recognized" to make such authoritative and binding legal determinations.

As EU integration moves forward and the Court of Justice gains prominence over an increasingly integrated Europe, the current and future constitutional status of secession will reveal whether the EU is grounded in the consent of its members or the coercive powers of centralized authority. Neither US nor EU high courts are tolerant of legal pluralism on the fundamentals, especially in the jurisprudential realm of rights. As the major thrust of international law is fueled by the policy quest for uniformity in the area of human and economic rights, national obstacles to the imposition of international standards are being overcome.

Two recent US Supreme Court cases, incorporating EU case law, manifest the trend towards an international case-law uniformity, through which national standards are circumvented and displaced by transnational norms. The decisions void state anti-sodomy statutes and capital felonies for anyone under eighteen.

In *Lawrence v. Texas,* writing for the majority, Justice Kennedy maintained:

> Of even more importance, almost five years before *Bowers* was decided the European Court of Human Rights considered a case with parallels to *Bowers* and to today's case. An adult male resident in Northern Ireland alleged he was a practicing homosexual who desired to engage in consensual homosexual conduct. The laws of Northern Ireland forbade him that right. He alleged that he had been questioned, his home had been searched, and he feared criminal prosecution. The court held that the laws proscribing the conduct were invalid under the European Convention on Human Rights. *Dudgeon v. United Kingdom,* 45 Eur. Ct. H. R. (1981) ¶52. Authoritative in all countries that are members of the Council of Europe (21 nations then, 45 nations now), the decision is at odds with the premise in *Bowers* that the claim put forward was insubstantial in our Western civilization.[77]

Furthermore, Justice Kennedy acknowledged that there is a sort of jurisprudential dialogue between the EU and US in the articulation of human rights. The US Supreme Court case *Bowers v. Hardwick* was deemed to be out of step with Western civilization and therefore overturned and replaced with the EU Court of Human Rights precedent:

"To the extent *Bowers* relied on values we share with a wider civilization, it should be noted that the reasoning and holding in *Bowers* have been rejected elsewhere. The European Court of Human Rights has followed not *Bowers* but its own decision in *Dudgeon v. United Kingdom.*"[78]

In *Roper v. Simmons,* the US Supreme Court announced that "the evolving standards of decency that mark the progress of a maturing society" result in a new understanding of the Eighth Amendment to the Constitution. The new understanding now deems as "cruel and unusual punishment" executing capital felons who committed their crimes while they were under the age of eighteen. The new understanding was aided by "other nations that share our Anglo-American heritage, and by leading members of the Western European community."[79] After citing the International Covenant on Civil and Political Rights, the United Nations Convention on the Rights of the Child, the American Convention on Human Rights, the African Charter on the Rights and Welfare of the Child, and the international community, Justice Kennedy concludes, "It is fair to say that the United States now stands alone in a world that has turned its face against the juvenile death penalty. . . . It is proper that we acknowledge the overwhelming weight of international opinion against the juvenile death penalty."[80]

Roper v. Simmons is a recent example of the US Supreme Court utilizing case law of the emerging world order, through which the policy preferences of international elites are imposed upon the American people, both nationally and within their respective States. One can only surmise that if US national statutes are judicially determined to be contrary to international standards, the US Supreme Court is able and willing to incorporate international standards into US case law.

Will international opinion and legal standards undermine US nationalism, as US nationalism undermined States' rights? The domestic political class that supports the UN Charter, its declarations and protocols, and the incorporation of international human-rights standards into US case law is determined to shape the American rule of law according to global standards. As for the self-determination of Missourians[81] who supported the criminal code that permitted the execution of Mr. Simmons for a horrendous, premeditated murder, Justice

Kennedy's rationale and the international standards he relies upon manifest only contempt.

American elites have adopted the standards of their international counterparts. As case law makes clear, they are able and willing to impose those standards upon the American people, just as the Lincoln Republicans imposed their standards, i.e., interest, upon the Confederacy. This is why both the US and CSA framers opposed a centralized union and favored a States' rights democracy, and why the present generation should oppose centralization whenever and wherever it rears its head. Centralization is inevitably the enemy of liberty, and liberty the enemy of tyranny.

Chapter V

SECESSION:
LIBERTY'S SAFEGUARD

The great rule of conduct for us, in regard to foreign nations is, in extending our commercial relations, to have with them as little political connection as possible. So far as we have already formed engagements, let them be fulfilled with perfect good faith. Here let us stop.

Pres. George Washington,
Farewell Address, September 1796

⊹ I ⊱

It is indisputable that an important motive behind the secession of Southern States from the Union was to decentralize power from the US government back to the States. This motive is evidenced by the act of secession itself and the decentralized nature of the CSA Constitution. In a very substantial way, the war between Northern (US) and Southern (CSA) States was a war over the centralization of political power. But centralization, like the Union itself, is a means to an end. The end is political power. The juxtaposition of political power and secession is just as significant today as it was in the 1860s, if not more so. As States' rights have suffered under the weight of national centralization, the nation is vulnerable to a similar fate under the pressures of transnational (or global) centralization.

This shift is reflected by the displacement of the word *international* (i.e., among nations) by the word *transnational* (i.e., above nations). As non-governmental organizations (NGOs) and intergovernmental organizations (IGOs) assume legal personalities in international law and politics, nations are losing their unique and exclusive standing in international matters. Nations now compete and cooperate with organizations such as Amnesty International and the World Trade Organization.[1]

Many of the unfolding events pertaining to the emerging world order will shock those who still adhere to the pre-World War II model of the law of nations, i.e., only nations have standing in international courts. But assuredly, the Anti-Federalists States' rights advocates of 1789 would be similarly shocked by the scope and reach of the US government's power over the States. The rule of law was crucial in the evolution of the latter by criminalizing secession and thereby sanctioning national centralization. The rule of law is proving to be crucial in sanctioning transnational centralization to the point where the demise of nations seems to be both natural and inevitable. Transnational centralization is resulting in a form of governing by a remote and unaccountable transnational elite, just as national supremacy resulted in being governed by a remote and unaccountable national elite. The difference is one of degrees; the transnational elite is more obscure and unaccountable than its national counterpart.

Secession was and is the critical antidote to this sort of centralization and is key to recovering the principles of 1776, i.e., "government instituted to secure life, liberty, and property," deriving its "just powers from the consent of the governed."

Contrast the simplistic beauty of the 1776 principles to the UN Charter's mandate for international human rights, which is essentially a vehicle for significant redistribution of wealth by international policy elites. According to former UN General Secretary Kofi Annan, "Wherever we lift one soul from a life of poverty, we are defending human rights. And wherever we fail in this mission, we are failing human rights." The UN commissioner for human rights clarified the UN's agenda:

> Economic deprivation—lack of income—is a standard feature of most definitions of poverty. But this in itself does not take account of the myriad of social, cultural and political aspects of the phenomenon. Poverty is not only deprivation of economic or material resources but a violation of human dignity too.
>
> Indeed, no social phenomenon is as comprehensive in its assault on human rights as poverty. Poverty erodes or nullifies economic and social rights such as the right to health, adequate housing, food and safe water, and the right to education. The same is true of civil and political rights, such as the right to a fair trial, political participation

and security of the person. This fundamental recognition is reshaping the international community's approach to the next generation of poverty reduction initiatives.[2]

Of course, the mechanism for enforcing these fundamental rights is the United Nations, working through its subunit nations, IGOs and NGOs. For example, all parties to the 1948 UN Charter are legally committed to the charter's article 25: "Everyone has the right to a standard of living adequate for the health and well-being of himself and of his family, including food, clothing, housing and medical care and necessary social services, and the right to security in the event of unemployment, sickness, disability, widowhood, old age or other lack of livelihood in circumstances beyond his control."[3] These are fundamental rights, the violations of which are to be litigated in national and international courts.

❧ II ❧

A review of key international documents clarifies the role US and UN courts will play in the implementation of internationally recognized rights. The emerging role of the courts in these areas will transform the American rule of law in the twenty-first century and, upon implementation, negate popular control over significant portions of public policy.

This impending negation of domestic law is all the more probable because a major bulwark against the implementation of transnational standards was torn down when national judicial supremacy replaced judicial federalism. The Supreme Court's monopoly over the state courts presents a unique opportunity for the incorporation of UN recognized rights (i.e., global socialism) into the marrow of American public policy. Even though the US Supreme Court is constitutionally charged with the maintenance of the rule of law within the context of popular control, the shift from state-based popular control to nationally based elitism facilitates the displacement of popular control with control by international elites.

The UN Declaration of Human Rights, the International Covenant on Economic, Social, and Cultural Rights (ICESCR), and the International Covenant on Civil and Political Rights (ICCPR) do not bode well for popular control. Like ticking time-bombs, these documents are ripe for detonation by future US Supreme Court justices. A brief overview must suffice.

The preamble to the 1948 UN Declaration of Human Rights is applicable to "all members of the human family . . . the aspiration of the common people," and "the peoples of the United Nations." The significance of a UN that is representative of the "human family" as opposed to exclusively representing nations is that the former constitutes a higher standard that could exercise a style of international supremacy over national standards that deviate from acceptable universal norms. From a juridical perspective, the supremacy of universal standards over nation-based standards (not to mention state based) could be rationalized on the grounds that the peoples of all nations have been integrated through these UN documents into the "human family," a transcendent political unit in its own right.

There is longstanding precedent for this sort of integration. In 1793, Justice Wilson directly addressed a similar issue:

> This is a case of uncommon magnitude. One of the parties to it is a state; certainly respectable, claiming to be sovereign. The question to be determined is whether this state, so respectable, and whose claim soars so high, is amenable to the jurisdiction of the supreme court of the United States? The question, important in itself, will depend on others, more important still; and, may, perhaps, be ultimately resolved into one, no less radical than this—do the people of the United States form a nation?

Relying on the "We the People" phrase of the Constitution's preamble, Justice Wilson answered with an emphatic yes.[4]

Chief Justice Marshall, in the case that established national legislative supremacy over the States, deduced from the preamble's "We the People" that the national "government proceeds directly from the people and is ordained and established in the name of the people."[5] As the people of the States were integrated into the people of the United States—essentially a transfer of sovereignty from the States to the nation—the people of the world's nations could be integrated into the UN human family—once again, a transfer of sovereignty. The human family is sovereign, with the United Nations acting as its agent.

The momentum of national integration into the UN's human family got a major boost in 1976 from the ICESCR, the ICCPR, and the Optional Protocol. These UN agreements supplement the "moral force" of the 1948 declaration with "legal obligations."[6] The 1948 declaration may be the central document, but these subsequent documents function as legal clarifications and implementation guidelines.[7]

The ICCPR most directly subsumes national and state identities into that of the "human family." The document proclaims that "the equal and inalienable rights of all members of the human family is [*sic*] the foundation of freedom, justice and peace in the world." The potential impact for the US is the shifting of sovereignty away from the States and nation to the UN. The UN serves as the governing unit representing the human family and determining what is and is not a universal fundamental right. When those rights have been violated, national governments are responsible for providing an effective remedy. The fact that a remedy based upon international standards is an inherent right of the claimant, domestic law notwithstanding, is a significant development.

Moreover, the claimant need not be a citizen of the nation against which the claim is filed. Article 2 stipulates: "Each State Party to the present Covenant undertakes to respect and to ensure to *all individuals within its territory and subject to its jurisdiction* the rights recognized in the present Covenant, without distinction of any kind, such as race, colour, sex, language, religion, political or other opinion, *national or social origin* property, birth or other status [emphasis added]."[8] To remove distinctions between citizens and noncitizens in the legal entitlement of rights, article 26 of the ICCPR stipulates: "*All persons* [emphasis added] are equal before the law and are entitled without any discrimination to the equal protection of the law. In this respect, the law shall prohibit any discrimination and guarantee to all persons equal and effective protection against discrimination on any ground such as race, colour, sex, language, religion, political or other opinion, national, or social origin, property, birth, or other status."[9] The term "all persons" makes national equal-protection discrimination unlawful not only against noncitizens but also against illegal aliens. Membership in the human family, not national citizenship, is the basis of fundamental rights.

Part V of the ICCPR established the Human Rights Committee and procedures for an ad hoc Conciliation Commission. The committee consists of eighteen nationals,[10] who "shall serve in their personal capacity," national allegiances notwithstanding. To wit, "every member of the Committee shall, before taking up his duties, make a solemn declaration in open committee that he will perform his functions impartially and conscientiously," i.e., nationalistic biases are unacceptable. The committee serves as a court of last resort between litigants, after the committee has "ascertained that all domestic remedies have been invoked and exhausted."[11]

Following similar rules of procedure, a nation that acceded to the Optional Protocol to the ICCPR is open to claims by "individuals subject to its jurisdiction who claim to be victims of human rights violations."[12] In the absence of the Optional Protocol, an individual was dependent on another nation to file a claim on his behalf. For example, a noncitizen inhabitant of the US seeking protection against a state for rights violations would have to secure the assistance of a second nation to file a complaint. But under the Optional Protocol, the individual may directly file his claim before the Human Rights Committee.[13] This is a major departure from traditional international law that governed relations between nations, but not between individuals. This departure is the "real test of the effectiveness of a system of international protection for human rights." Traditionally, the individual had no *locus standi* (a right to appear in court) within the context of international law. But that traditional rule was premised upon the relevance of sovereign nation-states, a relevance no longer sustainable in a world where "a common standard of achievement for all peoples and all nations is the goal."[14]

⊰ III ⊱

Several points about these documents need to be emphasized. First, the guarantees against discrimination include public and private, governmental and non-governmental. Second, the reliance on the word *persons* is a direct link to the human family, ultimately superseding nations. Third, the American federal system of reserved powers to the States is negated theoretically and technically, as is evidenced by articles 28, 50, and 10 of the ICESCR, ICCPR, and Optional Protocol respectively, which stipulate that "the provisions of the present Covenant shall extend to all parts of federal States without any limitations or exceptions" (such as the Tenth Amendment to the US Constitution).

Nonetheless, the more immediate threat to state sovereignty in the US is domestic, not international, courts. The current prevailing political reality precludes any UN tribunal (whether the International Court of Justice or the Human Rights Committee) from directly implementing their "human family" agenda.[15] But this is not to say that the US does not have certain legal obligations as a consequence of ratifying these UN agreements, obligations enforceable in US courts. The ICCPR stipulates: "To ensure that any person whose rights or freedoms as herein recognized are violated shall have an effective remedy . . . by competent judicial, administrative or legislative authorities, or by any other competent authority provided by the legal system of the State [nation], and to develop the possibilities of judicial remedies."[16] It was the clear intent of the drafters of the ICCPR and the Optional Protocol to ensure injunctive relief through domestic courts first and foremost, leaving open the option of international remedies if domestic legal systems were to fail.[17]

In 1985 this intent was formalized by the UN General Assembly when it adopted the Basic Principles on the Independence of the Judiciary, thereby charging domestic courts with the jurisdiction and mandate to incorporate UN-recognized rights into national law: "Whereas the ICESCR and ICCPR both guarantee the exercise of those rights . . . Whereas frequently there still exists a gap between the vision underlying those principles and the actual situation, Whereas the organization and administration of justice in every country should be inspired by those principles, and efforts should be undertaken to translate them fully into reality, Whereas rules concerning the exercise of judicial office should aim at enabling judges to act in accordance with those principles, Whereas judges are charged with the ultimate decision over life, freedoms, rights, duties and property . . . "[18]

Moreover, former UN General Secretary Boutros Boutros-Ghali viewed the heightened role of nationally based judiciaries as not only essential, but inevitable and part of the "historical synthesis resulting from a long historical process": "To move from identifying inequality to rebelling against injustice is only possible in the context of a universal affirmation of the idea of human rights. Ultimately, it is this idea which allows us to move from ethical to legal considerations, and *to impose* value judgments and *judicial constraints* on human activity [emphasis added]."[19]

❧ IV ❧

When ideology and opportunity converge, the development of public policy is affected accordingly. Constitutional barriers are no match for ideologically driven judges determined to address political questions. History has shown that opportunities will be seized in order to implement ideologically derived policy objectives.[20] The American constitutional order is premised upon this postulate,[21] as is the traditional American rule of law. Significantly, a UN articulation of human rights has very few checks and very little balance. Especially problematical is that the rule of law[22] is readily used as cover for government by an unaccountable elite. When, in the absence of States' rights, US judicial, legislative, and executive elites support the same ideological policy agenda, the end result is unchecked centralized political power.

From a practical viewpoint, it appears to be quite a stretch to link the idealistic language of UN documents to US public policy, but there are theoretical and historical justifications for doing so. Just as nineteenth-century precedent legitimized national supremacy over the States—"the laws must be faithfully executed"—twentieth-century precedent legitimized a form of transnational supremacy over the States that has made the nation itself vulnerable to the powers of "external sovereignty."[23]

The first significant precedent legitimizing transnational supremacy was a 1920 case, *Missouri v. Holland.* At issue was the constitutionality of the 1916 treaty between the US and Great Britain and the Migratory Bird Treaty Act of 1918, the purpose of which was to execute the terms of the treaty. The State of Missouri maintained that the treaty and the statute were repugnant to the Tenth Amendment. Counsel for Missouri argued:

> The treaty-making power conferred on the President and Senate does not include the right to regulate and control the property and property rights of an individual state, held in its quasi-sovereign capacity. . . . The lack of legislative power in Congress to divest a state of its property right and control over the wild game within its borders cannot be supplied by making a treaty with Great Britain. . . . The treaty-making power of the national government is limited by other provisions of the Constitution, including the 10th Amendment. It cannot, therefore, divest a state of its police power, or take away its ownership or control of its wild game.[24]

The essential legal issue was "can a treaty validate an otherwise unconstitutional congressional statute?" For the court, Justice Holmes provided an emphatic yes.

Justice Holmes maintained that in those instances when the national interests are at stake, and in those matters that require national action, the power to secure those interests and execute the necessary action must reside somewhere. Because the States are unable to individually secure national interests, the power is conferred upon the national government, not necessarily by the Constitution but by the Court. He wrote:

> With regard to that [the 1916 treaty], we may add that when we are dealing with words that also are a constituent act, like the Constitution of the United States, we must realize that they have called into life a being the development of which could not have been foreseen completely by the most gifted of its begetters. It was enough for them to realize or to hope that they have created an organism; it has taken a century and has cost their successors much sweat and blood to prove they created a nation. The case before us must be considered in light of our whole experience, and not merely in that of what was said a hundred years ago. The treaty in question does not contravene any prohibitory words to be found in the Constitution. The only question is whether it is forbidden by some invisible radiation from the general terms of the 10th Amendment. We must consider what this country has become in deciding what that amendment has reserved.[25]

These few lines represent a jurisprudence that will prove to have a profound impact on the American constitutional order. The tenets of that jurisprudence are: (1) statutory and fundamental laws are organic in nature; (2) laws are to be circumstantially understood; (3) the Tenth Amendment is subject to a juridical sliding scale, whereby the reserved powers of the States may be contracted while those of "superior" governments are expanded; and (4) the US Supreme Court is empowered to keep the organism growing and healthy. The incorporation of UN-recognized fundamental rights is part and parcel of that growth, if the US Supreme Court so decides.

Foreign affairs enhance the opportunities for centralizing political power. The US Supreme Court has made it clear that States' rights do not apply in foreign affairs. In the words of Louis Henkin, "foreign relations are national relations."[26] And the emerging world order— through which nations are integrated into a universal human family— has little legal tolerance for a traditional understanding of American nationhood.

International law requires four conditions for nationhood. First, there must be a *people* who live together in a community; second, there must be a *country* with a recognized territory; third, there must be a recognizable *government* exercising authority; and fourth, there must be a *sovereign,* "independent of any other earthly authority."[27] The juridical logic of *Missouri v. Holland* complements these four conditions, whereas the original constitutional order with its deference to States' rights does not.

Under the original American constitutional order, there is not, in the strict sense, "a people who live together in a community." There are, however, fifty distinct peoples living in state-based communities. Collectively the States form a national community, of sorts. But each state has a recognizable government exercising substantial powers within a recognized jurisdiction. The States are sovereigns, although not completely independent of each other as long as they are members of the same Union. Even the arch-nationalist Chief Justice Salmon P. Chase understood this when he wrote, "The Constitution, in all its provisions, looks to an indestructible Union, composed of indestructible States."[28]

What Chief Justice Chase did not fully acknowledge is that indestructible States are not reducible to the status of administrative agents of the national government, but exercise meaningful sovereignty over designated areas of public policy.[29] But according to *Missouri v. Holland,* the demarcation between reserved state powers and delegated national powers is circumstantially arbitrary—in other words, political. Thus, the sovereignty of the States over their purely internal affairs is not contingent upon the rule of law, but upon the rule of political expediency, especially when "a national interest of very nearly the first magnitude is involved," as presumably was the case in protecting Canadian migratory birds.

The same logic could be applied to national sovereignty. One could argue that national sovereignty over purely internal affairs is not contingent upon the rule of law, i.e., the US Constitution, but upon the rule of political expediency, especially when an international "interest of the first magnitude is involved," presumably such as the many interests listed in the ICESCR and ICCPR.

✦   V   ✦

The constitutional implications of *Missouri v. Holland* were shortly thereafter expanded in *US v. Curtiss-Wright* (1936), when the Supreme Court augmented the powers of the US presidency in the international realm, thereby fulfilling the worst fears of the eighteenth-century Anti-Federalists and nineteenth-century Southern Confederates.

At issue was the constitutionality of Congress delegating law-making powers to the US president. If such delegation falls exclusively within the category of internal affairs, it would be unconstitutional. However, if it falls partially within the categories of both internal and external affairs, it is not open to constitutional challenge.[30] Grounding his reasoning not in the "provisions of the Constitution, but in the law of nations," Justice George Sutherland ruled that "the investment of the federal government with the powers of external sovereignty did not depend upon the affirmative grants of the Constitution."[31] The powers of external sovereignty passed from the Crown—that is, King George III—to the government of the United States, and then onto the office of the president of the United States.

Relying on his New Deal-inspired nationalistic interpretation of American history, particularly the Declaration of Independence,

Justice Sutherland maintained the myth that the States never were independent or free and that the American people existed only in the national aggregate. He argued:

> Rulers come and go; governments end and forms of governments change; but sovereignty survives. A political society cannot endure without a supreme will somewhere. Sovereignty is never held in suspense. When, therefore, the external sovereignty of Great Britain in respect to the colonies ceased, it immediately passed to the Union. . . . The Union existed before the Constitution . . . [it] was the sole possessor of external sovereignty. . . . Otherwise, the United States is not completely sovereign.[32]

To make the US completely sovereign, Justice Sutherland only had to build upon the case-law precedents of his predecessors.

One year after the *Curtiss-Wright* decision, the Court took the next step and freed the treaty-making powers of the presidency from Senate ratification. In *US v. Belmont*,[33] the Court elevated international executive agreements to the same Article VI "supreme law of the land" legal standing as treaties. Treaties and international agreements are now instruments of altering not only the relationship between the States' reserved and the US's delegated powers, but of committing the national and state governments to international legal obligations entered into by a self-determining US president and yet fully enforceable in US and transnational courts.

But this was precisely the point. The US was not designed to be "completely" sovereign, nor was it designed to confer King George-like powers on its president. Nevertheless, *Missouri v. Holland, US v. Curtiss-Wright,* and *US v. Belmont* sanction the expansion of national power beyond the framers' wildest nightmares. If the 1776 American revolutionaries are to be believed and King George III was a tyrant, then these decisions conferred tyrannical powers on the US presidency.[34]

❧ VI ❧

In conclusion, the case-law precedent established by the US Supreme Court to subordinate States' rights to national supremacy is conducive to subordinating national supremacy to transnational authorities. Although state court dockets are proportionately much more active today than they have ever been, the US Supreme Court ultimately makes final determinations as to what the law is. A similar relationship among the US Supreme Court, European Court of Justice, and UN International Court of Justice is beginning to emerge.[35] The awesome power of judicial review that has decisively trumped States' rights is now being turned towards national rights. The US Supreme Court is in a position to incorporate into US case law UN policy objectives that will decisively trump national sovereignty. And just as the use of national force against noncomplying States has received the sanction of US Supreme Court case law,[36] national noncompliance with UN policy objectives is vulnerable to a similar fate. Thus, the confluence of laws being formulated farther and farther beyond States' rights popular control, by national and transnational elites, does not bode well for genuine community self-determination within the context of States' rights federalism.

As jurisprudence has been essential in legitimizing national centralization, it will likely be instrumental in global centralization. And just as state supreme courts quietly bowed to the US Supreme Court, the US Supreme Court is posturing to bow before international courts and world opinion. As Justice Joseph Story insisted, it is the necessity of "uniformity"[37] that justifies centralization. But this begs the question: uniformity for whom and towards what objective? For Story it was the national government and its American empire; for twenty-first-century elites it is the world government and the imposition of the human family's fundamental rights.

American jurisprudence, which was originally designed to secure life, liberty, and property through the rule of law, may now utilize the rule of law to take away the same. There may soon be no room for community self-determination within the context of the rule of law in the house that US Supreme Court nationalists helped to construct. Is it unreasonable to anticipate that the American people will face the fate of the CSA? Will Americans be confronted with a twenty-first-century Mr. Lincoln speaking not to the US Congress, but to the UN General Assembly, rhetorically suggesting to nationalists compliance or conquest? To dismiss, mock, or ignore the question is to answer it.

George W. Bush in 2005 hinted at an answer when dedicating the

Abraham Lincoln Presidential Library and Museum: "Lincoln's career and contributions were founded on a single argument: *That there are no exceptions* to the ringing promises of the Declaration of Independence; that all of us who share the *human race* are created equal. . . . Whenever freedom is challenged, the proper response is to go forward with confidence in freedom's power [emphasis added]."[38] This sort of rhetoric would be well received by the UN as a mandate to secure what it considered to be the fundamental rights of all members of the human family, including the right to globally enforce the redistribution idealism of the UN Declaration of Rights.

To effectively implement redistribution of wealth on a global scale requires a level of centralized political power to execute its policies without the interference of national governments. This rationale has 1788 precedence, as expressed by Alexander Hamilton in his argument against confederacies and for centralized governments with direct authority over individuals. Hamilton argued for national supremacy in order to mitigate the influence of, if not eliminate, state governments as intermediaries between centralized authority and individuals. Of course, the bracketed insertions below are not in his original argument, but they are included to demonstrate the application of Hamilton's logic to contemporary developments:

> Military coercion has never been found effectual. It has rarely been attempted to be employed, but against the weaker members [nations]; and in most instances attempts to coerce the refractory and disobedient [nations] have been the signals of bloody wars in which one half of the Confederacy [world community] has displayed its banners against the other half. The results of these observations to an intelligent mind must clearly be this, that if it is possible at any rate to construct a federal [world] government capable of regulating the common concerns and preserving the general tranquility [of the human family], it must be founded . . . [and] must carry its agency to the persons of the citizens [of the world]. It [the United Nations] must stand in need of no intermediate [national] legislations, but must itself be empowered to employ the arm of ordinary magistrates [international courts] to execute its own legislations. The majesty of the national [United Nations] authority must be manifested through the medium of the [international] courts of justice.[39]

Hamilton's advice against using military coercion, but supportive of judicial tribunals to regulate the "common concerns and preserve the "general tranquility," is a lesson well learned by the promoters of both US national supremacy and world government. Unlike the case with the CSA, the American rule of law will be crushed not by invading armies in blue, but most likely by decrees from national courts willfully incorporating precedent from international courts of justice.

Under the CSA model of government, the American rule of law was firmly grounded in the popular control and consent of the governed, i.e., traditional American democracy. National elites were more effectively constrained behind the walls of checks and balances, separation of powers, and States' rights, including interposition and secession. Courts were genuinely dedicated to securing the common-law rights of life, liberty, and property, not according to an ideological agenda of a particular judge or judges, but according to what the law demands. Like all human institutions, the Confederate States of America had deficiencies in both form and practice. Nevertheless, the traditional American rule of law, a rule of law predicated upon the consent of the governed, was most secure in its decentralized system of government.

The superiority of the CSA model of government is becoming increasingly obvious in light of recent developments through which traditional American democratic principles are being subverted in order to conform to global standards of right and wrong. If traditional American States' rights democracy is to be recovered, the CSA needs to be taken seriously. The lessons to be learned from its rise and fall are important in understanding the fall of the United States of America and the American rule *of* law to the forces of the emerging world order and the rule *by* law.

NOTES

Introduction

1. See Alexander Hamilton, James Madison, and John Jay, *The Federalist Papers,* #10. This is a collection of eighty-five essays, written between October 1787 to August 1788, justifying ratification of the US Constitution. The essays took the nationalist position against the Anti-Federalist States' rights position.

2. See Donald S. Lutz, *The Origins of American Constitutionalism* (Baton Rouge: Louisiana State University Press, 1988), chapters 10, 11.

3. General Agreement on Tariffs and Trade, North American Free Trade Agreement, Central American Free Trade Agreement, and the Security and Prosperity Partnership,.

4. See Bertrand de Jouvenel, *On Power: The Natural History of Its Growth* (Liberty Fund Press, 1993). The 1648 Treaty of Westphalia is also instructive, as the initial attempt to form nation-states to promote a "Christian and Universal peace" (see *The Avalon Project at Yale Law School,* http://www.yale.edu/lawweb/avalon/westphal.htm).

5. *Konrad v. Germany,* application #35504/03, 2006, http://cmiskp.echr.coe.int/tkp197/view.asp?item=4&portal=hbkm&action=html&highlight=&sessionid=8691516&skin=hudoc-en.

6. Cited in George W. Carey and Bruce Frohnen, ed., *Community and Tradition: Conservative Perspectives on the American Experience* (Lanham, Md.: Rowman & Littlefield, 1998), 11-12.

7. Ibid., 11.

8. http://www.freerepublic.com/focus/news/828843/posts.

9. Hamilton, Madison, and Jay, #1.

10. Ibid.

11. Alexis de Tocqueville, *Democracy in America,* part II, book IV,

chapter vi; cited in F. A. Hayek, *The Road to Serfdom* (Chicago: University of Chicago Press, 1994), xli.

12. See Trevor Colbourn, *The Lamp of Experience: Whig History and the Intellectual Origins of the American Revolution* (Indianapolis: Liberty Fund, 1998), for the ideological motivations of the 1776 American revolutionaries. The parallels between the American 1776 and 1861 revolutionary leaders are indisputable.

13. See Thucydides, *The History of the Peloponnesian War.*

14. Transnational in contradistinction to international; the latter relies upon viable nation-states, whereas the former does not.

15. *Hickman v. Jones,* et al., 76 US (9 Wall.) 197 (1870) 200-201.

Chapter 1

1. For a more detailed analysis of the CSA Constitution, see Marshall DeRosa, *The Confederate Constitution of 1861: An Inquiry into American Constitutionalism* (Columbia: University of Missouri Press, 1991).

2. One legal scholar asserts that the CSA Constitution is "suspiciously like the federal Constitution in many details" (Lawrence M. Friedman, *A History of American Law,* 2d ed. [New York: Simon & Schuster, 1985], 342).

3. See John C. Calhoun, "A Discourse on the Constitution and Government of the United States" (1850), in *Union and Liberty: The Political Philosophy of John C. Calhoun,* ed. Ross M. Lence (Indianapolis: Liberty Fund Press, 1992), 79-284.

4. *Calder v. Bull,* 1 L. Ed. 648 (1798) 315.

5. Ibid., 316. Iredell, while a nationalist during the ratification debates, frequently took pro-States' rights positions as a Supreme Court justice; for example, he dissented in *Chisholm v. Georgia* (2 US [2 Dall.] 419 [1793]), arguing against a State being sued in a federal court without its consent. The rationale behind his dissent is reflected in the Eleventh Amendment, which belies the court's reasoning that the United States is an association of individuals first and foremost and one of States only coincidentally. The use of the pronoun "one" in that amendment's reference to "one of the United States" is obviously a reference to a state and not an individual.

6. President Lincoln's Inaugural Address, March 4, 1861; see Marshall DeRosa, ed., *The Politics of Dissolution* ((New Brunswick, N.J.: Transaction, 1998), 342.

7. Ibid.

8. The same commitment to States' rights is found in article II of the Articles of Confederation: "Each State retains its sovereignty, freedom and independence, and every Power, Jurisdiction and rights, which is not by this confederation expressly delegated to the United States, in Congress assembled." It is noteworthy that the powers were delegated to the Congress assembled, and not to the chief magistrate.

9. This was an important topic at the 1787 Philadelphia convention. The nationalist Gouverneur Morris commented that the difference between a "federal" and a "national" government is that the former is a "mere compact resting on the good faith of the parties" whereas the latter has a "compleat and compulsive operation" (Max Farrand, ed., *The Records of the Federal Convention,* vol. 1, 34 http://memory.loc.gov/ammem/amlaw/lwfr.html).

10. During the summer of 2004, the European Union intensely debated whether to include in its constitution's preamble a reference to God and Europe's Christian roots. On behalf of those members in support of the inclusion, the "Polish prime minister vowed to 'fight like lions' on the issue." Also in support of the reference, the Vatican "regretted the opposition of certain governments to a specific acknowledgement of Europe's Christian roots." The preference for a strictly secular preamble won the day, with France and Belgium arguing that such a reference would violate separation of church and state (http://www.christiantoday.com/news/eur/350.htm).

11. *McCulloch v. Maryland,* 4 L. Ed. 579 (1819).

12. Ibid.

13. See *Black's Law Dictionary,* 6th ed. (West, 1990).

14. See *Black's Law Dictionary* for the linguistic nuisances between the two terms.

15. It is notable that the CSA framers placed their version of the US Tenth Amendment in Article VI, as an explicit counterbalance to the supremacy clause.

16. *McCulloch v. Maryland.*

17. A "rule" is a "prescribed guide for conduct or action, regulation

or principle," whereas a "law" is ordained and established, in effect a statute; see *Black's Law Dictionary.*

18. The US legislatively mandated a similar budgeting and accounting process in 1921; see http://www.rules.house.gov/archives/jcoc2w.htm.

19. The US Constitution permitted the States, with congressional consent, to "lay any Imposts or Duties on Imports or Exports, except what may be absolutely necessary for executing its inspection Laws" (Article I, section 10, clause 2).

20. Similar reasons were behind the ratification of the Twenty-second Amendment to the US Constitution in 1951, which limited the US president to two four-year terms.

21. The impeachment proceedings in the House against Pres. Andrew Johnson would not have been possible in the CSA. President Johnson would have been able to purge his administration of Radical Republicans, if he desired to do so.

22. It is important to keep in mind that the CSA framers expected the Confederacy to expand, eventually including States northward along the Mississippi Valley and westward towards the Pacific. Their confidence in limited government and free trade led them to believe that many of the free States in the old Union would join in order to participate in the economic prosperity of the CSA, leaving the Northeastern States to wither on the vine of economic stagnation. Senators in those States shared that concern and bemoaned competing against their CSA rivals; see DeRosa, *The Politics of Dissolution.*

23. Richard Posner repeatedly and correctly contends that "state governments were (and are) more democratic than the federal government" (*Law, Pragmatism, and Democracy* [Cambridge, Mass.: Harvard University Press, 2003], 148).

24. *Journal of the Confederate Congress,* 1:7.

25. Ross M. Lence, ed., *Union and Liberty: The Political Philosophy of John C. Calhoun* (Indianapolis: Liberty Fund Press, 1992), 195.

26. Frank Moore, ed., *The Rebellion Record* (New York: G. P. Putnam's Son, 1863), 1:3.

27. Henry Steele Commager, ed., *Documents of American History* (New York: Appleton, Century, Crofts, 1963), 1:178-79.

28. Lence, 15.

29. Ibid., 26.

30. Moore, 1:37.

31. J. K. Spaulding, "State Sovereignty and the Doctrine of Coercion" (Charleston, 1860), 6, 28.

32. "In common usage the term is ordinarily used to describe that state of mind denoting honesty of purpose, freedom from intention to defraud, and, generally speaking, means being faithful to one's duty or obligation" (*Black's Law Dictionary*).

33. Daniel J. Elazar and John Kincaid, ed., *Covenant, Polity, and Constitutionalism* (New York: University Press of America, 1980), 11.

34. A. L. Hull, "The Making of the Confederate Constitution," *Southern Historical Society Papers* 28 (1900): 291.

35. Lence, 446.

36. *Annals of Congress of the United States* (Washington, DC: Gales and Seaton, 1834), 1:458.

37. Ibid., 1:452.

38. Jonathan Elliot, ed., *The Debates in the Several State Conventions on the Adoption of the Federal Constitution* (Salem, N.H.: n.p., 1987), 3:330. This is essentially Madison's "extended republic" argument; see Hamilton, Madison, and Jay, #10.

39. *Annals of Congress,* 1:800-801.

40. Article I, section 2, clause 5.

41. Article V.

42. Jefferson Davis, *The Rise and Fall of the Confederate Government,* 2 vols. (New York: D. Appleton and Company, 1881), 1:172-73.

43. The credentials of St. George Tucker as an authority on the meaning of the US Constitution are impeccable. In 1803 he published an expanded and annotated edition of William Blackstone's *Commentaries on the Laws of England.* Tucker became known as the American Blackstone. Recent editors note: "For lawyers and scholars alike, *Tucker's Blackstone* remains a key source for understanding how Americans viewed English common law in the years following the adoption of the Constitution and Bill of Rights" (*St. George Tucker's Blackstone's Commentaries,* Paul Finkelman and David Cobin, ed. [Union, N.J.: The Lawbook Exchange, 1996], i-ii).

44. St. George Tucker, *View of the Constitution of the United States; With Selected Writings,* Clyde N. Wilson, ed. (Indianapolis: Liberty Fund, 1999), 94).

45. *McCulloch v. Maryland* (1819) and *Gibbons v. Ogden* (1824); hence the New Deal, Great Society, and similar national intrusions into the States' reserved powers would be precluded.

46. *Cohens v. Virginia,* 5 L. Ed. 257 (1821) and *Martin v. Hunter's Lessee,* 4 L. Ed. 97 (1819).

47. *Texas v. White,* 74 US (7 Wall.) 700 (1869).

48. *Missouri v. Holland,* 64 L. Ed. 641 (1920).

49. *US v. Curtiss-Wright,* 299 US (1936).

50. *Engel v. Vitale* (1962) and *Lemon v. Kurtzman* (1971).

51. *U.S. Term Limits, Inc. v. Thornton* (1995).

52. *US v. Carolene Products Co.* (1938), *Griswold v. Connecticut* (1965), *Roe v. Wade* (1973), *Lawrence v. Texas* (2003).

Chapter 2

1. Brian Z. Tamanaha, *On the Rule of Law: History, Politics, Theory* (New York: Cambridge University Press, 2004), 3.

2. Hayek, 80.

3. A. V. Dicey, *Introduction to the Study of the Law of the Constitution,* 10th ed. (New York: St. Martin's Press, 1965), 183-283.

4. According to Michael Oakeshott, Europeans as well as Americans are somewhat perplexed by the concept: "The rule of law is a common expression. It is often used, somewhat capriciously, to describe the character of a modern European state or to distinguish some states from others. More often it appears as a description of what a state might perhaps become, or what some people would prefer it to be" (Michael Oakeshott, *On History and Other Essays* [Indianapolis: Liberty Fund, 1999], 129).

5. Hamilton, Madison, and Jay, #10.

6. See Arthur R. Hogue, *Origins of the Common Law* (Indianapolis: Liberty Press, 1985), 53-55.

7. Tamanaha, 15.

8. Over the centuries the English developed a court system that was so complex and cumbersome that Sir Edward Coke dedicated the fourth volume of his *Institutes* to characterizing it. See Friedman, 37.

9. John Maxcy Zane, *The Story of Law* (Indianapolis: Liberty Fund, 1998), 335.

10. Ibid., 249.

11. The transition from the US to the CSA legal system was designed to be one of continuity, as the fifth act of the CSA Provisional Congress, on February 9, 1861, stipulated that "all the laws of the United States of America, in force and in use in the Confederate States of America on the first day of November last, and not inconsistent with the Constitution of the Confederate States, be and the same are hereby continued in force until altered or repealed by the Congress" (*Journal of the Confederate Congress,* 1:41). The *Journal* makes it unquestionably clear that the CSA was formed by and operated under the highest parliamentary standards. See the *Journal of the Confederate Congress* for examples of these high standards (http://memory.loc.gov/ammem/amlaw/lwcc.html).

12. John Pendleton Kennedy, *Swallow Barn: Or A Sojourn in the Old Dominion* (Baton Rouge: Louisiana State University Press, 1986), 9-10. Kennedy's first edition was published in 1832. When the second edition was published in 1853, he included the cited comments to note the changes that had occurred in Virginia over the past twenty years.

13. Mark E. Neely, *Southern Rights: Political Prisoners and the Myth of Confederate Constitutionalism* (Charlottesville: University Press of Virginia, 1999), 9-10.

14. Ibid., 132-33.

15. Scholarship hostile to the CSA points to the lack of case-law reports as evidence that courts within the CSA were tantamount to vigilante justice, a vigilantism particularly tough on slaves and poor whites. What that scholarship fails to mention is the extreme paper shortages that made it almost impossible to record case law. However, the lack of a paper record is not evidence that civil and criminal procedures were not followed.

16. See William M. Robinson, *Justice in Grey: A History of the Judicial System of the Confederate States of America* (Cambridge, Mass.: Harvard University Press, 1941), 83-88.

17. See *Black's Law Dictionary.* The impressment of private property for such purposes dates back to national independence. Tory properties confiscated by the States during the Revolutionary War were to be returned to the owners, as stipulated in postwar treaties. Nevertheless, the States in the postwar era were reluctant to comply. When the US Supreme Court decision *Chisholm v. Georgia* (1793])

opened US courts to Tory suits seeking to recover properties, Massachusetts governor John Hancock convened a special session of the state legislature to propose a constitutional amendment that was swiftly ratified as the Eleventh Amendment to the US Constitution. That amendment effectively placed Tory suits in state courts, thereby providing the States with more control over the suits. See Charles Warren, *The Supreme Court of the United States: In Two Volumes, 1789-1835,* vol. 1 (Boston: Little, Brown, 1926), 99-100.

18. See *Black's Law Dictionary.*

19. *Lee v. Munroe,* et. al., 11 US 366, 7 Cranch 366 (1813).

20. *Journal of the Confederate Congress,* 3:209.

21. Ibid., 3:189.

22. Ibid., 3:352.

23. *William H. Tyson v. Harrison Rogers,* 33 GA 473 (March 1863).

24. A possessory warrant is a summary remedy for the recovery of personal property that has been taken by fraud, violence, enticement, or seduction from the possession of the complaining party (see *Black's Law Dictionary*).

25. *Tyson v. Harrison,* 3.

26. *Cox & Hill v. Cummings,* 33 GA 549 (July 1863).

27. Ibid., 5-6.

28. Ibid., 6-7.

29. Ibid., 7. It is interesting that the seized sugar did not fall into the category "absolute necessity or great public utility" when it was essential to the war effort in what Lumpkin described as "the death-struggle in which our people are engaged" (*Cox & Hill v. Cummings,* 6). The emergency threshold was high, indeed.

30. Ibid., 9.

31. Ibid.

32. *Hardie C. Cunningham v. David L. Campbell,* et al., 33 GA 625 (1863).

33. Ibid., 3, 4.

34. Ibid., 3.

35. Ibid., 3-4.

36. Ibid., 8.

37. Ibid., 7.

38. Ibid., 9.

39. Ibid., 10.

40. *Benjamin F. White v. Joseph B. Ivey* and *Benjamin F. White v. A. C. Pease, Agent of J. T. Reese,* 34 GA 186 (1865).

41. *White v. Ivey,* 9.

42. Ibid., 9-10.

43. Ibid., 10.

44. *David L. Yulee v. Major Atonia A. Canova, CSA,* 11 FL 9 (1865).

45. Sugar was a very important commodity during the war, second only to cotton in economic terms but primary, perhaps, for the military commissaries. See Charles P. Roland, *Louisiana Sugar Plantations During the Civil War* (Baton Rouge: Louisiana State University Press, 1997).

46. Ibid., 5.

47. Ibid.

48. Ibid., 22.

49. Ibid., 30.

50. Ibid., 31.

51. "Just compensation means an equivalent, a recompense in value for the property taken, what the article would sell for in the market, quality and quantity considered, and not the price which the owner might demand, or some person for especial reason might be willing to give" (Ibid., 33).

52. Ibid., 34.

53. See *Black's Law Dictionary.*

54. Article I, section 9, clause 3.

55. *Journal of the Confederate Congress,* 1:660.

56. Ibid., 2:26. The expiration provision was added by the Congress on April 19, 1862. The Congress twice renewed the suspension.

57. Ibid.,2:445.

58. *In the Matter of J. C. Bryan,* 60 NC 1 (1863), 1.

59. The military manpower shortages were acknowledged by both sides to be severe.

60. *Bryan,* 4.

61. Ibid., 9.

62. Ibid., 10.

63. Ibid., 11, 12.

64. *State, ex rel. Dawson, in re Strawbridge & Mays,* 39 AL 367 (1864),

25. The 1864 law modified 1862 and 1863 laws. (Note: *Ex rel.* indicates that the proceedings include parties that have an interest in the case. In this particular case, it meant that the state was representing Dawson's legal interests.)

65. Ibid., 4.
66. Ibid., 6.
67. Ibid.
68. Ibid., 14.
69. Ibid., 14-15.
70. Ibid., 19-20.
71. Ibid., 21.
72. Ibid., 23.
73. Ibid., 27-28.
74. *Burroughs v. Peyton* and *Abrahams v. Peyton,* 57 VA 470 (1864).
75. *Burroughs,* 2.
76. Ibid., 3-4.
77. Ibid., 10.
78. Ibid., 9.
79. Ibid., 4-5.
80. Ibid., 6.
81. Ibid., 5.
82. *John Barnes v. John T. Barnes,* 53 NC 366 (1861).
83. Ibid., 3.
84. Ibid., 4.
85. Ibid., 4-5.
86. *Juaraqui v. The State,* 28 TX 625 (1861), 1-2.
87. See John Remington Graham, *Blood Money: The Civil War and the Federal Reserve* (Gretna, La.: Pelican, 2006).
88. *Journal of the Confederate Congress,* 4:572.
89. *Josephine v. Mississippi,* 39 MS 613 (1861).
90. Ibid., 10. The legal issues were more complex and numerous than the ones summarized here.
91. Ibid., 21.
92. Ibid., 20.
93. *Elvira,* 57 VA 561 (1865), 3-4.
94. Ibid., 5.
95. *Jones & Daugharty v. Aaron Goza,* 16 LA Ann. 428 (1862), 1-2.

Chapter 3

1. "Franklin Pierce: His Qualifications for, and Pretensions to, the Presidency," *The American Whig Review* 95 (November 1852), 390.

2. Larry Gara, *The Presidency of Franklin Pierce* (Lawrence: University Press of Kansas, 1991), xi.

3. See Hamilton, Madison, and Jay, #47, for James Madison's explanation of how the accumulation of legislation and judicial functions in the same hands results in tyranny.

4. Academic admirers of Lincoln not only acknowledge that his policies and rhetoric remade the constitutional framework, but applaud the displacement of the rule *of* law by the rule *by* law; see Garry Wills, *Lincoln at Gettysburg: The Words That Remade America* (New York: Simon & Schuster, 1992) and George P. Fletcher, *Our Secret Constitution: How Lincoln Redefined American Democracy* (New York: Oxford University Press, 2001).

5. See M. E. Bradford, "Lincoln, the Declaration, and Secular Puritanism: A Rhetoric for Continuing Revolution," in *A Better Guide Than Reason: Federalists and Anti-Federalists* (New Brunswick, N.J.: Transaction, 1994), 185-203.

6. See Thomas J. DiLorenzo, *The Real Lincoln: A New Look at Abraham Lincoln, His Agenda, and an Unnecessary War* (Roseville, Calif.: Prima, 2002).

7. Mario Cuomo, *Why Lincoln Matters Today More Than Ever* (New York: Harcourt, 2004), 27, 28.

8. Ibid., 169-70.

9. Our working definition of the rule of law is "the absolute supremacy or predominance of regular law as opposed to the influence of arbitrary power, and excludes the existence of arbitrariness, of prerogative, or even of wide discretionary authority on the part of government" (Hayek, , 80). Based upon this definition, which is the only one consistent with original American understanding of the role of government, President Pierce is to be lauded for his commitment to the rule of law.

10. *The American Presidency Project* (Santa Barbara: University of California), http://www.presidency.ucsb.edu/site/docs/doc_platforms.php?platindex=D1852.

11. Walter M. Merrill, *Against Wind and Tide: A Biography of Wm. Lloyd Garrison* (Cambridge, Mass.: Harvard University Press, 1963), 205.

12. *The American Presidency Project,* http://www.presidency. ucsb.edu/site/docs/doc_platforms.php?platindex=R1856.

13. *The Avalon Project.*

14. See *Journal of the Senate of the United States of America, 1789-1873,* Second Session of the Thirty-third Congress, January 3, 1855, 79-91, for President Pierce's veto message to the Congress and a concise yet superb statement of government under the constitutional constraints (http://memory.loc.gov/cgi-bin/ampage).

15. Gara, 107.

16. See *Prigg v. Pennsylvania,* 16 Pet. (41 US) 539 (1842), and *Ableman v. Booth,* 21 Howard (62 US) 506 (1859); these two cases manifest an ongoing reluctance in the Northern States to comply with fugitive slave laws.

17. Avery Craven, *The Coming of the Civil War,* 2d ed. (Chicago: University of Chicago Press, 1957), 337.

18. Susan-Mary Grant, *North Over South: Northern Nationalism and American Identity in the Antebellum Era* (Lawrence: University Press of Kansas, 2002).

19. Ibid., 123.

20. Craven, 469.

21. *Journal of the Senate,* January 3, 1855, 82.

22. Ibid., 79.

23. Ibid., 90.

24. Ibid., 81-82.

25. See *Prigg v. Pensylvania.*

26. Article IV, section 2, clause 3, stipulates, "No person held to Service or Labour in one State, under the Laws thereof, escaping into another, shall, in Consequence of any Law or Regulation therein, be discharged from such Service or Labour, but shall be delivered up on Claim of the Party to whom such Service or Labour may be due."

27. Massachusetts Personal Liberty Act of 1855, http://usinfo. state.gov/usa/infousa/facts/democrac/20.htm.

28. According to one biographer, Cushing was one of the most influential members of Pierce's administration. He was "by far the

most learned and well-traveled member of the cabinet" and Pierce "leaned heavily on his advice" (Gara, 69).

29. Claude M. Fuess, *The Life of Caleb Cushing,* 2 vols. (Hamden, Conn.: Archon, 1965), vol. ii, 181-82. Cushing submitted to President Pierce a detailed account of the statutory and customary responsibilities of the attorney general. His recommendations were accepted by the president and transformed the office: "Cushing's exhaustive analysis of the origin and duties of his position has been accepted by later incumbents as constituting the authoritative statement on the subject, and ought to be viewed as a notable public document. Cushing was, as this document clearly shows, the highest type of public servant,—intelligent, industrious, tireless, systematic, progressive, and interested in his routine and special work" (ibid., 182). Cushing's antebellum commitment to the rule of law was revisited by Republicans when President Grant nominated him as the chief justice to the US Supreme Court. His nomination was withdrawn when it became obvious that it would be defeated on "purely partisan grounds" (ibid., 376). In other words, for Republican senators, it was political payback time; Cushing's refusal to capitulate to political pressure when he served as Pierce's attorney general cost him the chief justiceship of the US Supreme Court.

30. United States Attorney General, *Official Opinions of the Attorneys General of the United States: advising the President and heads of departments in relation to their official duties* (Washington, D.C.: R. Farham, 1852-70), 302.

31. Ibid., 303.

32. Ibid., 306.

33. Ibid.

34. Ibid.

35. *New York Daily Times,* 23 March 1853, 4.

36. See Grant, 61-80.

37. Justice Campbell suffered a political fate similar to President Pierce: "His moderate stance on slavery alienated Southerners, while his proslavery opinion in the *Dred Scott* case outraged many Northerners. By 1860, Campbell found himself in the unenviable position of a moderate seeking accommodation between irreconcilable factions" (Kermit L. Hall, ed., *The Oxford Companion to the Supreme*

Court of the United States [New York: Oxford University Press, 1992], 117).

38. *Scott v. Sandford,* 19 Howard (60 US) 393 (1857). Scott was taken by his owner into Illinois, which prohibited slavery, and territory north of the 36 degrees 30 minutes Missouri Compromise line. Scott's counsel maintained that Scott's residence in free territory made him a free man, even after his return to Missouri, where slavery was sanctioned.

39. Section 8 stipulates, "And be it further enacted. That in all that territory ceded by France to the United States, under the name of Louisiana, which lies north of thirty-six degrees and thirty minutes north latitude, not included within the limits of the state, contemplated by this act, slavery and involuntary servitude, otherwise than in the punishment of crimes, whereof the parties shall have been duly convicted, shall be, and is hereby, forever prohibited: Provided always, That any person escaping into the same, from whom labour or service is lawfully claimed, in any state or territory of the United States, such fugitive may be lawfully reclaimed and conveyed to the person claiming his or her labour or service as aforesaid" (Conference committee report on the Missouri Compromise, March 1, 1820; Joint Committee of Conference on the Missouri Bill, 03/01/1820-03/06/1820; Record Group 128l; Records of Joint Committees of Congress, 1789-1989; National Archives).

40. See note 26 above. Justice Campbell's analysis of Lord Mansfield's jurisprudence regarding the Somersett case (involving the legal status of a Virginian slave transported to England by his owner in 1770) is of particular relevance to the situation in the US, where state liberty laws were used to obstruct the enforcement of national fugitive slave laws. See *Scott v. Sandford,* 496-501.

41. *Scott v. Sandford,* 509.

42. Ibid.

43. Ibid., 515-16.

44. Ibid., 512.

45. See DeRosa, *The Politics of Dissolution, inter alia,* for how prominent the compact theory of the Union was for the Democrats, and how committed the Republicans were to displace it with a union of US citizens. The former is essential to States' rights, whereas unfettered national supremacy depends upon the latter.

46. *Carter v. Carter Coal Company,* 298 US 238 (1936).

Chapter 4

1. The concept *imperial rule* is meant to imply a system of governing in which the locus of sovereignty is not limitable, but extends and retracts its influence based upon its perceived interests. Nevertheless, its natural inclination is towards expansion.

2. Paolo G. Carozza, "Subsidiarity as a Structural Principle of International Human Rights Law," *The American Journal of International Law* 97, no. 38 (2003): 52.

3. Theodor Schilling, "Subsidiarity as a Rule and as a Principle, or; Taking Subsidiarity Seriously" (New York: New York University School of Law Jean Monnet Center, 1995), http://www.jeanmonnet-program.org/papers/95/9510ind.html#I.

4. Carozza, 40.

5. Europa glossary, http://europa.eu/scadplus/glossary/subsidiarity_en.htm.

6. The draft EU Constitution, http://europa.eu.int/constitution/en/fpart4_en.htm.

7. European Convention, July 18, 2003, http://eur-lex.europa.eu/smartapi/cgi/sga_doc?smartapi!celexapi!prod!CELEXnumdoc&lg=en&numdoc=52003XX0718(01)&model=guichett.

8. Hamilton, Madison, and Jay, #39.

9. EU Constitution, Title I, article 3(b).

10. Ibid., Title V, article 1-29, 3(a).

11. Ibid., Title IX, article 1-60.

12. This process is well under way. See Darcy S. Binder, "The European Court of Justice and the Protection of Fundamental Rights in the European Community: New Developments and Future Possibilities in Expanding Fundamental Rights Review to Member State Action" (New York: New York University School of Law Jean Monnet Center, 1995), http://www.jeanmonnetprogram.org/papers/95/9504ind.html.

13. *Texas v. White,* 74 US (7 Wall.) 700 (1869).

14. See International Court of Justice, http://www.icj-cij.org/icjwww/icjhome.htm. The International Court of Justice is the principal judicial organ of the United Nations. It began work in 1946, when it replaced the Permanent Court of International Justice, which

had functioned since 1922. It operates under a statute largely similar to that of its predecessor, which is an integral part of the UN Charter.

15. James M. Buchanan, "Federalism, Liberty and the Law," in *The Collected Works of James M. Buchanan,* vol. 18 (Indianapolis: Liberty Fund, 2001), 104-5.

16. This in no way is meant to imply that Southerners acted unconstitutionally when they seceded from the Union. To the contrary; secession was and to a certain extent remains a constitutional prerogative of the States. For a comprehensive analysis, see John Remington Graham, *A Constitutional History of Secession* (Gretna, La: Pelican, 2002).

17. The rule of law is defined as: "A legal principle, of general application, sanctioned by the recognition of authorities, and usually expressed in the form of a maxim or logical proposition. Called a 'rule,' because in unforeseen cases it is a guide or norm for their decision" (*Black's Law Dictionary,* 6th ed. [1990]).

18. Coercion has many manifestations, ranging from physical force (e.g., relying on the president to use or threaten to use the resources of his office to enforce a court order) to institutional usurpation (e.g., the manipulative use of judicial review to enhance institutional power).

19. Over the past several centuries, the vitality of arbitrary power has grown commensurate with so-called democratic institutions, particularly in Europe. See de Jouvenel.

20. See "EU Constitution: Where Member States Stand," BBC News, July 7, 2005, http://news.bbc.co.uk/1/hi/world/europe/3954327.stm.

21. See William Lasser, *The Limits of Judicial Power: The Supreme Court in American Politics* (Chapel Hill, N.C.: University of North Carolina Press, 1988).

22. John McCormick, *Understanding he European Union: A Concise Introduction,* 2d ed. (New York: Palgrave, 2002), 109.

23. State-based popular control and popular consent constitute the essence of early American political and constitutional developments. See Donald S. Lutz, *Popular Consent and Popular Control: Whig Political Theory in the Early State Constitutions* (Baton Rouge: Louisiana State University Press, 1980). In 1847, the US Supreme Court defined state popular sovereignty as a state's police powers. These are state powers to "govern men and things within the limits of its own dominion"

(License Cases, 5 Howard [46 US] 504 [1847]). The States' police powers provided policy jurisdiction over the health, safety, and morals of their respective citizens.

24. See *Cohens v. Virginia* and *Martin v. Hunter's Lessee*.

25. EU Constitution, Title IV, chapter I, article 1-29, http://europa.eu/constitution/en/ptoc5_en.htm#a25.

26. The EU's policies of direct effect and the primacy of community law are much more specific than the interpretative gymnastics utilized to convert Article I, section 8, congressional commerce powers into the carte blanche of national supremacy. See Gavin Smith, *The European Court of Justice: Judges or Policy Makers?* (London: Bruges Group, 1990). Moreover, the four main categories of EU law (regulations, directives, decisions, and recommendations) provide the European Court of Justice with ample materials to construct a uniquely European rule of law jurisprudence.

27. The operative word is "constitutionally," which would include procedures recognized by all member States as legitimate and compliant with the rule of law.

28. The steady stream of Supreme Court case law that flows through the US Union seems unremarkable, following the ancient riverbeds confirmed by the US Constitution, e.g., the Article VI supremacy clause. Due in large measure to its reliance on selectively using precedent and politically astute incrementalism, Supreme Court case law has increased national judicial power in a way that appears legitimate. But behind the scenes, forceful changes to the American system of federalism have occurred under the guise of the American rule of law as articulated by the US Supreme Court. Specifically, the flow of American case law has substantially altered the landscape of the union of States and the popular control of government it was designed to ensure. Moreover, this current landscape is increasingly inhospitable to the Jeffersonian tree of liberty, which requires a viable federalism conducive to meaningful States' rights policy options. State supreme courts were part and parcel of States' rights policy options vis-à-vis the national government. Without such options, how are state-based popular control and popular consent to be preserved in a union? See chapter 14, "The Right of Resistance: Secession and the Modern State," in Donald W. Livingston's *Philosophical Melancholy and Delirium: Hume's Pathology of Philosophy* (Chicago: University of Chicago Press, 1998).

29. Alexis de Tocqueville, *Democracy in America,* George Lawrence, trans.; J. P. Mayer, ed. (New York: Harper & Row, 1969), 114-15.

30. *St. George Tucker's Blackstone's Commentaries,* i-ii.

31. Tucker, 94.

32. The states are Virginia, New York, and Rhode Island. See H. Newcomb Morse, "The Foundations and Meaning of Secession," *Stetson Law Review* xv (1986): 429.

33. See Forrest McDonald, *States' Rights and the Union: Imperium in Imperio, 1776-1876* (Lawrence: University Press of Kansas, 2000). McDonald convincingly dispels the myths that the Union preceded the States, that the locus of sovereignty was initially in the Union, and that the primacy of the Union is buttressed by the supremacy clause.

34. See chapter 2 of DiLorenzo and see also DeRosa, *The Confederate Constitution of 1861.*

35. See DiLorenzo.

36. McDonald, 87.

37. Ibid., 84-96.

38. Ibid., 72.

39. Ibid., 193.

40. For a concise treatment of Lincoln and the war, see DiLorenzo, especially chapter 6.

41. McDonald, 231.

42. License Cases, 5 Howard (46 US) 504 (1847).

43. See Daniel J. Elazar, *Building Toward Civil War: Generational Rhythms in American Politics* (Lanham, Md.: Madison Books, 1992).

44. The Supreme Court may indeed determine what the law is, but its determination, although constitutional, may be erroneous. Thus, if one agrees with Chief Justice Marshall that "it is emphatically, the province and duty of the judicial department, to say what the law is" (*Marbury v. Madison,* 5 US 137 [1803]), then compliance with an erroneous determination by the court is required. The court by definition cannot make erroneous decisions, unless the court concedes as much in subsequent rulings.

45. I do not mean to imply that for secession to be legitimate it must be in response to tyranny. Perhaps secession should not be taken for "light and transient causes," as the Declaration of Independence admonishes. However, as an important component of popular sovereignty, a state is not precluded from seceding for less weighty reasons.

46. As posited by Hamilton, "It has frequently been remarked that it seems to have been reserved to the people of this country, by their conduct and example, to decide the important question, whether societies of men are really capable or not of establishing good government from reflection and choice, or whether they are forever destined to depend for their political constitutions on accident and force" (Hamilton, Madison, and Jay, #1).

47. *Texas v. White,* 725.

48. Tocqueville, 368.

49. William Rawle, *A View of the Constitution of the United States of America,* 2d ed. (Philadelphia: Phillip H. Nicklin, 1829), 142. This book was widely used in legal education, including at West Point until 1840.

50. Ibid., 142.

51. These safeguards found their way into the US Constitution due, in large measure, to the abuses the colonists endured by the Crown while asserting their rights under the English system.

52. Article III, section 3.

53. See Graham, *A Constitutional History of Secession,* chapter 2, for the relevance of 1776 precedent.

54. The ordinance was ratified on February 23, 1861, by a vote of 46,153 to 14,747.

55. *Texas v. White,* 718.

56. Ibid., 722, 724.

57. Ibid., 725.

58. *Luther v. Borden,* 7 Howard (48 US) 1 (1849), concerns the constitutional meaning of the "guaranty clause" in Article IV, section 4, which stipulates, "The United States shall guarantee to every State in this Union a Republican Form of Government, and shall protect each of them against Invasion; and on the Application of the Legislature, or of the Executive (when the Legislature cannot be convened) against domestic Violence." In 1842, Rhode Island's Dorr Rebellion had raised the issue of the meaning of "a Republican Form of Government." Dorr and his supporters (primarily from the growing urban areas) established a state government in protest against the incumbent government (dominated by rural interests). Martial law was declared and resulted in litigation between Mr. Luther, a Dorr partisan, and Borden, a state militiaman enforcing martial law.

59. *Texas v. White,* 729.

60. Ibid., 721.

61. Ibid., 730.

62. *Luther v. Borden,* 42.

63. *The Congressional Globe,* March 15, 1861, 1441.

64. Ibid., 1442.

65. *The Constitution of the State of Texas As Amended in 1861: Address to the People,* Austin, March 30, 1861, 4.

66. *Texas v. White,* 727-28.

67. Ibid., 729.

68. Ibid., 733.

69. Tucker, 22.

70. *Texas v. White,* 734.

71. Ibid., 725-26.

72. In civil law, "incorporation" is the union of one domain to another (*Black's Law Dictionary*).

73. *Texas v. White,* 726.

74. Ibid., 740.

75. "Free Masonry and the War: Report of the Committee Under the Resolutions of 1862, Grand Lodge of Virginia, in Reference to Our Relations as Masonic Bodies and as Masons, in the North and South, Growing out of the Manner in Which the Recent War has been Prosecuted. Adopted by the Grand Lodge of Virginia, December 12, 1864, and ordered to be published. John Dove, Grand Secretary" (Rare Book Collection, UNC-CH, call number 5102 conf.).

76. See Hamilton, Madison, and Jay, #1.

77. *Lawrence v. Texas* (June 26, 2003; slip opinion), 12.

78. Ibid., 16.

79. *Roper v. Simmons,* US Supreme Court, No. 03-633 (2005 US Lexis 2200), 6 of 58.

80. Ibid., 13-14 of 58.

81. In addition to Missouri, Alabama, Arizona, Arkansas, Delaware, Florida, Georgia, Idaho, Kentucky, Louisiana, Mississippi, Nevada, New Hampshire, North Carolina, Oklahoma, Pennsylvania, South Carolina, Texas, Utah, and Virginia permitted the imposition of the death penalty on juveniles seventeen and eighteen years old.

Chapter 5

1. These organizations number in the hundreds; for a list of IGOs see http://www.library.northwestern.edu/govinfo/resource/internat/igo.htm l and for NGOs see http://www.summit-americas.org/NGOlist2.htm.

2. Office of the United Nations High Commissioner for Human Rights, http://www.ohchr.org/english/issues/poverty/index.htm.

3. UN Declaration of Rights, http://www.unhchr.ch/udhr/lang/ eng.htm.

4. See *Chisholm v. Georgia* (1793).

5. See *McCulloch v. Maryland* (1819).

6. See *The International Covenants on Human Rights and Optional Protocol* (New York: UN Office of Public Information, 1976), 1. It declares, "Having proclaimed this Universal Declaration [1948], the UN turned to an even more difficult task: transforming the principles into treaty provisions which established the legal obligations on the part of each ratifying State." The US Senate ratified the ICCPR and Optional Protocol in 1992. To date, the ICESCR has not been ratified by the Senate; however, that does not preclude its terms from influencing American jurisprudence as components of the customary law of nations.

7. See Imre Szabo, "The Historical Foundations of Human Rights and Subsequent Developments," in *The International Dimensions of Human Rights,* vol. 1, ed. Karol Vasak (Westport, Conn.: Greenwood Press, 1982), 23.

8. ICCPR, 13, 14.

9. Ibid., 22.

10. The term *national* in this context is broader than the term *citizen;* see *Brassert v. Biddle,* DC Conn., 59 F. Supp. 457, 462 (*Black's Law Dictionary*).

11. ICCPR, 28, 38, 41.

12. Optional Protocol to the ICCPR, article 1.

13. See part IV of the ICCPR.

14. A. H. Robertson, "The Implementation System: International Measures," in *The International Bill of Rights: The Covenant on Civil and Political Rights,* ed. Louis Henkin (New York: Columbia University Press, 1981), 357, 365.

15. For example, the ICESCR delineates the fundamental rights that members must respect, including: the right of all people to self-determination (art. 1); the equal right of men and women to the enjoyment of all economic, social, and cultural rights (art. 2); the right to work and the right to freely choose or accept the work one does (art. 6); the right to favorable working conditions, fair wages, leisure, and paid holidays (art. 7); the right of everyone to form a trade union, the right of trade unions to form national federations, the right of national federations to form international trade-union organizations, the right to strike (art. 8); the right of everyone to social security and social insurance (art. 9); the right of everyone to an adequate standard of living and the fundamental right to be free from hunger (art. 11); the right of everyone to the "enjoyment of the highest attainable standard of physical and mental health" (art. 12); and "the right of everyone to education" (art. 13).

16. ICCPR, 2.

17. See Oscar Schachter, "The Obligation to Implement the Covenant in Domestic Law," in *The International Bill of Rights,* 325.

18. Office of the United Nations High Commissioner for Human Rights, http://www.unhchr.ch/html/menu3/b/h_comp50.htm.

19. Boutros-Ghali, Boutros, *The United Nations and Human Rights: The United Nations Blue Book Series,* vol. 7 (New York: United Nations Department of Public Information, 1995), 442-43.

20. Marshall L. DeRosa, *The Ninth Amendment and the Politics of Creative Jurisprudence: Disparaging the Fundamental Right to Popular Control* (New Brunswick, N.J.: Transaction, 1996).

21. "If the impulse and opportunity be suffered to coincide, we well know that neither moral nor religious motives can be relied on as an adequate control. They are not found to be such on the injustice of individuals, and lose their efficacy in proportion to the number combined together, that is, in proportion as their efficacy becomes needful" (Hamilton, Madison, and Jay, #10).

22. What is meant by the traditional rule of law cannot be easily explained, but only appreciated; in other words, it is less abstraction and more procedure. For example, the rule of law does not necessarily require that a US president serve a four-year term instead of a five-year term. Article V of the Constitution allows for the change from four- to

five-year terms. Rather, the rule of law requires that the length of the term be determined by constitutional procedures, such as the amendment process and not congressional statute of judicial decree.

23. This term was coined by Justice Sutherland and is discussed later in this chapter.

24. *Missouri v. Holland,* 64 L. Ed. 641 (1920) 645.

25. Ibid., 648.

26. Louis Henkin, *Foreign Affairs and the Constitution* (Mineola, N.Y.: Foundation Press, 1972), 228.

27. These four conditions are a slight variation of those found in L. Oppenheim's *International Law: A Treatise,* vol. 1, ed. I. H. Lauterpacht (New York: David McKay, 1962), 118-19.

28. *Texas v. White,* 725.

29. "The powers not delegated to the United States by the Constitution, nor prohibited by it to the States, are reserved to the States respectively, or to the people" (Tenth Amendment).

30. *US v. Curtiss-Wright,* 315-16.

31. Ibid., 303.

32. Ibid., 302-3.

33. *US v. Belmont* 301 US 324 (1937). The legislative response to this decision was headed by US Sen. John Bricker, a conservative Republican from Ohio. Senator Bricker unsuccessfully proposed a series of constitutional amendments, the last one in 1956. It stipulated: "Section 1. A provision of a treaty or other international agreement not made in pursuance of this Constitution shall have no force or effect. This section shall not apply to treaties made prior to the effective date of this Constitution. Section 2. A treaty or other international agreement shall have legislative effect within the United States as a law thereof only through legislation, except to the extent that the Senate shall provide affirmatively, in its resolution advising and consenting to a treaty, that the treaty shall have legislative effect. Section 3. An international agreement other than a treaty shall have legislative effect within the United States as a law thereof only through legislation valid in the absence of such an international agreement. Section 4. On the question of advising and consenting to a treaty, the vote shall be determined by yeas and nays, and the names of the Senators voting for and against shall be entered on the Journal of the Senate"

(Duane Tannanbaum, *The Bricker Amendment Controversy: A Test of Eisenhower's Political Leadership* [Ithaca, N.Y.: Cornell University Press, 1988], 227).

34. See the Declaration of Independence and Hamilton, Madison, and Jay, #1.

35. See *Mexico v. United States of America* (Case Concerning Avena and Other Mexican Nationals), International Court of Justice (March 31, 2004), General List No. 128.

36. See *Martin v. Hunter* and *Texas v. White*.

37. Ibid., 346.

38. *President Dedicates Abraham Lincoln Presidential Library and Museum,* April 19, 2005, http://www.whitehouse.gov/news/releases/2005/04/20050419-5.html.

39. Hamilton, Madison, and Jay, #16.

Index